BRISTOL'S
BASTARDS

BRISTOL'S BASTARDS

IN IRAQ WITH THE
2ND BATTALION, 136TH INFANTRY
OF MINNESOTA'S NATIONAL GUARD

Nicholas P. Maurstad & Darwin Holmstrom

ZENITH PRESS

First published in 2008 by Zenith Press, an imprint of MBI Publishing Company,
400 1st Avenue North, Suite 300, Minneapolis, MN 55401 USA.

Zenith Press titles are also available at discounts in bulk quantity for industrial or sales-promotional use. For details write to Special Sales Manager at MBI Publishing Company, 400 1st Avenue North, Suite 300, Minneapolis, MN 55401 USA. To find out more about our books, join us online at www.zenithpress.com.

Designer: Diana Boger

ON THE COVER: A simulated IED emits a firestorm as soldiers in the Iowa National Guard's 1st Battalion, 133rd Infantry, experience the concussion and noise of an explosion during Theater Immersion Training at Camp Shelby, Mississippi, early 2006. The Iowa unit rounded out the 1st Brigade, 34th "Red Bull" Division, of nearly four thousand soldiers that served in Iraq. *U.S. Army*

ON THE BACK COVER: The squad poses for a picture for the Patriot Guard to say thank you for the commemorative shirts they are wearing in front of their company mural, while Yogi (upper right) makes a statement about life in Camp Taqaddum.

Unless otherwise noted, all photos © Nicholas P. Maurstad

Library of Congress Cataloging-in-Publication Data

Maurstad, Nicholas P., 1985-

Bristol's bastards : in Iraq with the 2nd Battalion, 136th Infantry of Minnesota's National Guard / Nicholas P. Maurstad and Darwin Holmstrom. -- 1st ed.

  p. cm.

ISBN 978-0-7603-3277-1 (hb w/ jkt)

1. Iraq War, 2003---Personal narratives, American. 2. Maurstad, Nicholas P., 1985- 3. Soldiers--United States--Biography. I. Holmstrom, Darwin. II. Minnesota. National Guard. III. Title.

DS79.76.M385 2008

956.7044'342092--dc22

[B]
          2008023130

Printed in the United States of America

For all the good soldiers and marines
I served with in Iraq, especially
Corey, Bryan, and Jimmy.

Contents

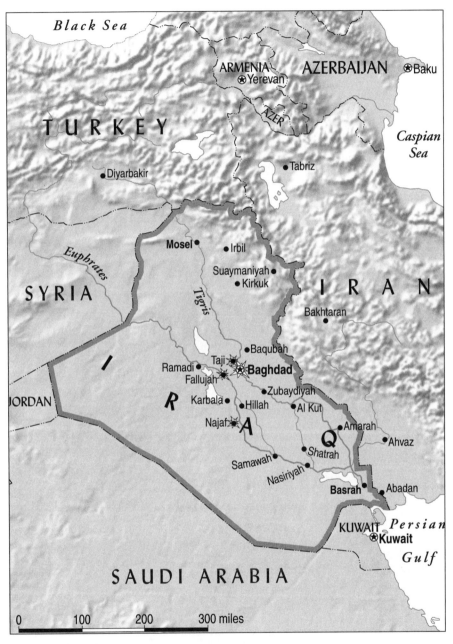

Iraq and surrounding countries. *Phil Schwartzberg, Meridian Mapping*

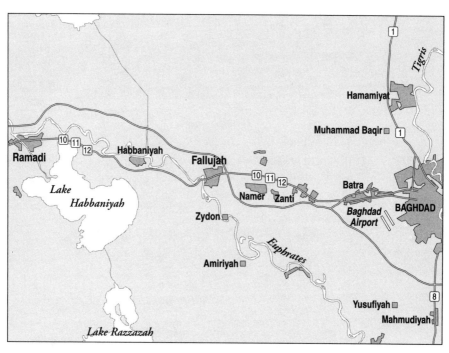

Area of operations. *Phil Schwartzberg, Meridian Mapping*

I must say, I'm a little envious. If I were slightly younger and not employed here, I think it would be a fantastic experience to be on the front lines of helping this young democracy succeed. It must be exciting for you . . . in some ways romantic, in some ways, you know, confronting danger.

—George W. Bush, March 13, 2008

Right now I'm in Iraq, in support of Operation Iraqi Freedom. This is definitely not the most glorious place in the world, but there's no other place I would rather be. Putting everything on the line to defend my country is something I wanted to do and am proud to be here. My family means the world to me! They have always stood behind me with every decision in my life. I don't know where I would be without them.

—Bryan McDonough, December 1, 2006

Never explain.

—Hunter S. Thompson, frequently

Nick "Winnie" Woinarowicz eats a cup of noodles. Ramen is gourmet food compared to MREs.

January 9, 2007

E VERYONE GET THE FUCK OUTSIDE!" Sergeant Jay Horn, our team leader, yelled from the hallway.

The tone of his voice frightened me. He sounded frantic and worried. My gut told me something awful had just happened. I looked at Winnie. In addition to being a fellow member of the Barbarians (Bravo Company of the 2-136 Infantry of the Minnesota National Guard), Winnie—Nick Woinarowicz—married my second cousin Amanda Maurstad about one month before we left for Iraq, which made him family. His face told me that he was nervous too.

He'd never seen Horn spaz like this before and knew that whatever had his undies in a bunch couldn't be good. After everything that had happened, we expected the worst, but right now we didn't need the worst. We only had to survive thirty more days in Anbar Province, where we were conducting combat patrols southeast of Fallujah along the Euphrates River. After that we had thirty more days to finish our mobilization order, and then we'd finally go home. We didn't need to deal with another death.

We walked to the porch outside our barracks. It was the place we gathered to get information. A grim Sergeant First Class Erik Myrold, our piece-of-shit temporary platoon sergeant while Sergeant First Class Michael Rogers was home on emergency leave, stood in front of the group.

Once everyone arrived, Myrold said, "We just received word that 1st Squad hit a VBIED [vehicle borne improvised explosive device, which is military clusterfuck language for 'car bomb'] during a foot patrol in al Zanti." Zanti,

1

Scott "Grub" Grabowska shows off his porn-star mustache in the motor pool.

one of the bigger Iraqi villages located about two miles southeast of Pump House Flanders (which we often used as our patrol base), was populated by people whose opinions of us ranged from indifference to homicidal rage. "All we know right now is that there is one guy that is urgent surgical and there are some other injuries that are not specific."

Myrold told us to stay around the barracks and wait for more information, so I went back to my room with Winnie. I finished making the bean and bacon soup I'd opened just before we heard Horn yelling.

I ate my soup while Winnie and Scott "Grub" Grabowska, my bunkmate from Goodrich, Minnesota, talked about how they hoped everyone would be okay. They consoled themselves with talk about how lucky it was that more people weren't seriously injured by the car bomb. I didn't have much to add to the conversation. I didn't feel like we'd been all that lucky.

An hour later Myrold called us back out to the porch. "It has just been confirmed that Sergeant Wosika was killed this afternoon. It was a stationary

Jimmy "Sika" Wosika has a smoke in Kuwait.

VBIED that Sika [our nickname for Jimmy Wosika] walked up to check out when it was remotely detonated. If anyone needs to talk tonight, I will be available and so will Lieutenant Blomgren."

Sergeants Jake Brown and Brian Micheletti, members of Jimmy's squad, were standing next to me. I gave them both hugs and comforted them, just as they had comforted me a month earlier when our squad had been hit.

The platoon followed Lieutenant Wade Blomgren to the motor pool to meet 1st Squad as they came back home. We met Colonel George Bristol and Sergeant Major Walter O'Connell in the motor pool when we got there. They walked through the crowd giving us hugs and talking to us, making sure we were going to be okay.

When 1st Squad drove in, Jimmy's squad leader Staff Sergeant Kelly Jones met them in our motor pool. We called Jones "Old Balls," because he was the quintessential crusty old army sergeant, a former U.S. Army Ranger with gigantic Ranger balls.

Staff Sergeant Kelly "Old Balls" Jones becomes saltier by the second in the Iraqi desert.

The rest of the platoon let the members of 1st Squad talk for a minute, and then walked over to see them. We knew what they were going through. We helped the guys out of their body armor, took the machine guns off of the humvees, and put tarps over the humvees to keep rain and dust from falling in through the turret. When all of the trucks were taken care of, we helped the guys carry their gear back to the barracks.

I experienced a powerful sense of déjà vu. Once again, about half the platoon stayed outside on the smoking porch behind our barracks. Almost everyone was smoking, even people who didn't smoke, but I managed to refrain from lighting up. I stayed out with everyone even though I didn't feel like talking about anything because I didn't want to be anywhere by myself.

We'd learned the ritual by now and knew what to do next without being told. Once again we walked to the tent next to the morgue. When we arrived Jimmy was already inside on the table. I walked in near the back of the platoon, doing my best to let the others who knew him better stand in front of me.

I found a spot to stand where I could see through the small crowd and saw Jimmy on the table. It disturbed me to see the outline of the body bag. When I saw my friend lying on the same table a month earlier, it didn't look much different from him lying in a sleeping bag. Jimmy's bag was mostly flat at one end and suddenly turned into a large lump in the middle.

The chaplain gave a prayer and said some words about Jimmy. When the chaplain finished, he told us that we could touch Jimmy's head and have a moment with him before we left.

The group stood for a minute in silence. Then one at a time we put our hand on Jimmy and said our goodbyes. I took my turn in the middle of the group. I put my hand on the bag where I was told his head was. I looked down at him for a minute and could only think about what an asshole I was for not having any emotion.

I left the tent upset that I was unable to shed a tear for Jimmy. I felt completely empty inside. I'd already cried enough for other friends who'd died and I just didn't have anything left to feel for Jimmy.

A few hours later, we gathered at the helicopter pad to send another of our dead brothers home. The experience was eerily similar to what happened after our squad was hit a little more than a month earlier; here we were again. I stood in the line forming the gauntlet with my back to the helicopters as they landed. The wind nearly blew me over, and the pebbles and sand kicked up by the wind stung my legs and back.

A four-man detail carried Jimmy to the helicopter; we saluted as his body went by, and the helicopter hovered for a minute before it flew into the darkness. Then Jimmy was gone. The only thing I found different was, instead of sadness, I felt completely numb.

Once again we would have to go back the very next day to the place where our friend had died. Blomgren selected our squad to gather intelligence in the village where he was killed. Dave, a young Iraqi 'terp (we called the interpreters who worked for us "'terps"), volunteered to be our 'terp. Dave was one of our best 'terps and he and Jimmy had been close friends; he wanted vengeance.

Second Squad walking through the wasteland southeast of Fallujah.

We drove to Flanders in the early afternoon, dropped off our trucks, and walked the two miles to Zanti.

We first walked through Namer, another fairly large village located about halfway between Zanti and Flanders, cursing the civilians as we passed. Every time I saw an Iraqi face, rage and hatred filled me. They were the first emotions I'd felt since I'd learned Jimmy had died and I wanted to hang onto them, even if they made me want to destroy everything I saw.

We crossed a small bridge and entered Zanti from the north. I walked near the back because I was in charge of a three-man team responsible for gathering detainees and holding them.

I watched the soldiers in front of me as they came to the first adult male in the village. At least he was adult in the Iraqi sense of the word; he looked about fifteen years old and was scared shitless. Dave walked to the front of the pack and, without saying a word, choke-slammed the poor guy. Dave had been one of the most professional Iraqis working for us and had been pretty easygoing until then, but he'd seen his close friend die the day before and he went completely apeshit on the kid. The rest of the team walked past while Dave yelled at him. Then Dave let him up, grabbed another guy, and started to throw him around. We moved through the village violent and fast.

Within fifteen minutes every man in the village lay face down in a field. Dave interrogated them one by one while I stood guard over them, making sure they did not speak to one another or try to escape. The women and children in the village cried and screamed in the distance. They hadn't seen us with such aggressive attitudes before.

After the interrogation was underway, I had a couple of other guys guard the Iraqis in the field while I walked over to look at the spot where the car bomb had killed Jimmy the day before. Nothing remained of the car other than some scattered pieces and the front axle. Horn came over and said, "Jones is on the other side of the canal looking for Jimmy's arm. They said they didn't find it last night. Will you help him look for it? Keep an eye on Jones while you're at it."

I walked in the weeds growing along the opposite side of the small canal, shadowing Old Balls. He and Jimmy had been close, and he was taking Jimmy's death hard. A little ways down from the black spot on the ground that used to be a car bomb. I found Winnie staring at the ground. I stood next to him and saw that he was looking at the place where Jimmy had died. We stood there for a minute or two looking at the bloody grass.

"That's so fucked up," I said, breaking the silence.

"No shit," Winnie added.

"Let's get out of here," I told him. "We don't want to look at this for too long."

"You're probably right," he said. I turned to keep searching for my friend's missing appendage. Winnie followed me and we talked a little bit to keep our mind off of the work.

After walking a couple of hundred meters, I fell and plugged the barrel of my M4 with mud. I sat down with Winnie and we talked while I used his cleaning kit to clean out my weapon. I ran the cable snake through the barrel a couple of times, making sure there was no debris in the barrel, and then we started walking again. We took our time because I knew there was some bad shit going on during the interrogation and I didn't want to know about it.

We walked back to the road where Dave was just finishing his interrogation. The Bradleys waited on the road while Captain Charles "Chip" Rankin, Bravo Company's commander, passed some of the intelligence gathered that day to the command center. He wanted to raid a village that had been identified as the source of the car bomb. We were all itching for the opportunity to meet the people who'd killed our friend and return the favor.

Colonel Bristol denied us the opportunity. It was late in the day and we lacked the manpower to safely carry out the mission, so he ordered us not to go. I suspect that Bristol knew what we would do to the bastards responsible for killing Jimmy, because he wanted to do the same. He and Jimmy had been close. Jimmy had been a state champion wrestler at Highland Park Senior High, and Bristol was a black belt in judo and the person who had started the Marine Corp Martial Arts Training Program (MCMAP). Jimmy and Bristol had been part of a group of soldiers who got together at the gym each week to wrestle and practice martial arts. Bristol knew we would slaughter the people who'd killed Jimmy because he'd do the same if he got his hands on them. He held us back to avoid another Haditha-like massacre.

That night, back on base, I called my family. We talked for nearly two hours, which meant I was on the phone for four hours due to a thirty-minute time limit. My last phone call was to my father at about one in the morning.

"How are you doing?" my dad asked.

"Not doing very good. We lost another guy in my platoon yesterday," I replied, choking on my words.

"I'm sorry, bud. I wish I knew what to tell you."

"It's okay. I just wanted to say that I am okay and that it isn't anyone you know. I can't tell you any more than that."

"Well I am happy that you're okay. I know it is a shitty way to look at it, but you only have about thirty days of work left, and you'll be on your way home in sixty days. I can't even imagine how hard it must be for you right now, but if you keep looking at the finish line, it might make it a little more bearable."

"I can see what you're saying. It just sucks having to keep going out there everyday and wonder if it will be me next. I've got to go. I need to get some sleep."

"Okay, kid. If there is anything you need, just call."

"All right. I love you, Dad."

"Love you too, kid. I'll talk to you later."

"Yeah, bye Dad." I hung up the phone and walked out back to my barracks, trying to face my own mortality. It took me the whole ten-minute walk to calm down. When I got to the door of my room I was feeling a lot better, understanding that I just had to get myself through the next month and I would be fine.

I opened the door and found Grub in his bed, watching Wolf Blitzer on CNN. When I got into the room I was so lost in my own thoughts that Blitzer's voice was just white noise, but before I could unsling my rifle his words started to sink in: "The plan outlined in the surge calls for four brigades to be mobilized earlier than expected and one Minnesota National Guard brigade already in Iraq to be extended for an extra four months."

I looked at Grub for a minute to make sure I had really heard what Blitzer had just said. His face confirmed that I was not hallucinating. "Fuck!" I yelled. I wheeled around and left the room, slamming the door.

I walked around our compound for a few minutes and began to laugh. I had six months left in this filthy fucking gravel pit, six months of getting shot at, dodging IEDs, and tolerating the stench of shit that permeated the entire country. I laughed so hard I nearly pissed myself. It occurs to me now that might have been the moment I became an unhinged sociopath—that is, the moment I became the perfect soldier.

CHAPTER 1:
Enlisting

I CELEBRATED MY NINETEENTH BIRTHDAY in the front leaning rest position at Fort Benning, Georgia. The front leaning rest position isn't nearly as comfortable as it sounds. In fact, it is not a rest position at all; it's military double-speak for a pushup position, which, by definition, is the polar opposite of "rest." I was in this position because my group had failed to complete the impossible task our drill sergeants had given us. It was my first day of basic training, and I was trying to figure out how I had gotten to this point.

I'd just spent eleven days in reception, a euphemism for the purgatory where the army sent me while I waited to begin basic training. There I was inoculated against every bug and virus known to medical science and a few I suspect were made up because some rear echelon motherfucker was getting a fat kickback from the pharmaceutical company selling the vaccine, the end result of which will likely be that any children I may have will be flipper babies. Then I was issued my uniforms, robbed of my hair, and stripped of my individuality. On the morning of my birthday, January 16, 2004, I was marched from reception to Sand Hill, where the U.S. Army trains all of its infantry recruits.

I felt like I was in a movie as I made the mile-long march, a bad movie with cliché characters—sadistic drill sergeants, naïve farm kids, urban thugs, incompetent officers, and a buxom milkmaid to serve as the love interest. I met most of those stereotypes at Fort Benning, except for the milkmaid. That part is poetic license on the part of the filmmakers; in real life a soldier's only love interest is usually connected to his wrist.

We walked down a hill and saw the training areas full of people practicing everything from hand-to-hand combat to drill and ceremony marching. Every thirty or forty seconds, I heard groups of two or three explosions in the distance. We marched past a big wooden sign that said "Welcome to Sand Hill, Home of the Infantry" and onto the lawn in front of our barracks.

Earlier in the morning we had loaded our sea bags onto one of four trucks, and now we stood in formation in front of four piles of fifty sea bags. Our impossible task was to find our individual bags in the piles and return to formation with them within three minutes.

Drill Sergeant Disque looked at his watch, picked up the megaphone he'd been using to torture us with all morning, and ordered us to pick up our bags. I ran to my pile and dug for my bag like a dog trying to escape from a fenced-in backyard. I didn't know what I was doing, so I followed the only advice my friend Trevor, who had joined the national guard six months before I did, gave me about basic training: "Don't ever be last."

I found my bag and made it back to my spot well before Disque blew the whistle signaling that our time was up. More than half of the privates failed to find their bags, so Disque ordered us back into formation and explained the proper way to do a pushup. Before I knew it I found myself in front leaning rest trying to figure out how I ended up in such a position.

■

As a six-year-old I watched the first Gulf War on television with my father. I didn't understand what was happening, but I was aware that there was a war and that the American army was winning. As I grew older I became more interested in current events and always seemed more concerned with what was going on in the world than the other kids in my hometown of Newfolden, a small town (population 384) in northwest Minnesota.

I lived the first eighteen years of my life on a farm twelve miles west of town, and my dad raised me to be a hard-working kid.

When I was in kindergarten my parents divorced. It was okay for a year or two; my parents were civil to each other and my dad would even let my mom come and stay with us on the farm for the weekend while he went fishing. I thought things were going well and enjoyed being raised by my dad and my grandparents, who lived across the road.

My dad re-married the month before I started the second grade. I liked having a mother around everyday again. My stepmother had three kids of her own, two boys and a girl who was the same age as me. The oldest one was really cool, until he started drinking and became violent. The other son was borderline retarded with a hair-trigger temper. My stepmom pretended he wasn't a psychotic retard, but she must have suspected that the boy wasn't quite right because she spoiled him rotten.

At first my father's new wife acted like the model stepmom, but as time went on, she slowly turned into a horrendous bitch. I realized that she was crazy just after my twelfth birthday. I told her that I wanted to go to my great grandmother's funeral. In an attempt to alienate me from my mother, she said, "You don't need to go to that funeral. She wasn't really your grandmother anyway," implying that somewhere along the line, someone in my mom's family had been a bastard. I was forbidden to attend the funeral.

As the years passed, she got more abusive. I'm not talking about run-of-the-mill evil-stepmother abuse, either; I'm talking about full-bore psychological warfare type operations designed to break the spirit of me, my brother, and my sister. For example, she punished us for bed-wetting by making the perpetrator sit naked in the kitchen for the entire morning while the other five kids got ready for school. She once even tried to make my sister eat her own vomit, but my father intervened and stopped her.

She was not a stupid woman, and she used every intellectual resource available to conceive punishments designed to rob us of any shred of self-esteem. Things were different when it came to her kids. For example, she dismissed the sexual molestations committed by her borderline-retarded son as youthful pranks, but when it came to me, my brother, and my sister, she pursued our complete psychological annihilation with the zeal of a Pentecostal missionary, and she was damn good at it.

She was such a master of deceit and manipulation that whenever we tried to tell our dad about what was going on, she'd convince him that we were lying and that we were deeply disturbed and needed psychological help for thinking up such twisted shit in the first place. If he did intervene, she'd back off momentarily, only to retaliate with ten times as much force when he thought the situation had been resolved. This woman was so deep-down awful that her actions probably deserve to be chronicled in a book of their own, but nothing would make the attention-starved torture beast happier than to be the subject of a book, so I'm going to plagiarize a line from *Forrest Gump*: "That's all I have to say about that."

After my sophomore year in high school, I got a summer job working eighty hours a week for a stereotypical Norwegian bachelor farmer and spent whatever free time I had with my steady girlfriend, in order to avoid spending time at home with my sociopathic stepmother.

But I lived in the same house as the bitch and couldn't avoid her completely. In a misguided attempt to disguise the fact that she constantly tortured my brother, sister, and me, she made a public spectacle of being involved in our lives. She forced me to play high school sports even though I was arguably the worst athlete on every team. Unfortunately, in a school that small, the athletic department needed every warm body it could get its hands on just to fill a team's bench; a total lack of skill or talent wasn't enough to keep a person off of any team for which he or she tried out. And I had a total lack of skill or talent in all sports. My body seemed to reject sports with a pair of, what an observer-controller in Camp Shelby would later describe as "weak-assed bitch ankles." Add to that a pair of knees that wouldn't stay in the right configuration even if they were bolted in, and the result was a basketball player with a total of twelve points for his freshman year.

I spent my entire thirteen years in school pissing away potential. I consistently scored among the top of my class in tests, proving that I had the capacity to be an A student. My lack of a drive to succeed, coupled with low self confidence, turned me into a person who didn't earn a lot of respect. Most people wrote me off as a failure before I even graduated. My principal, Mr. Thygeson, even suggested that I apply at McDonald's because that was as far as I was ever going to get in life.

My stepsister tried to join the Minnesota National Guard during the summer before our senior year. Our family knew that she wouldn't ever really do it, and if she actually did try, her excessive weight would probably keep her out. She kept trying to join well into our senior year before finally giving up.

Her attempts to join the national guard got me interested in joining. I was following the war in Afghanistan with great interest, just as I had followed the Kosovo conflict a few years earlier. I watched footage of American troops patrolling the streets of Kandahar and Kabul on CNN during study hall and

The Bradley Fighting Vehicle that I wanted to drive, which was the reason
I joined the national guard. I didn't get to drive one for the first four years of
my service.

wondered if I could do such a difficult and honorable job. I wanted people to
respect me the same way I respected the men on TV.

One day I walked into the guidance counselor's office on a whim, pointed
to a picture of a Bradley fighting vehicle, and said, "I want to drive that." He
told me about different job options, college benefits, and bonuses. I listened
for about five minutes before I stopped him, saying, "I just want to join the
infantry and drive a Bradley." Surprised at how easily he had just picked up a
recruit, he set up an appointment with my parents and shoved me out of the
office before I could change my mind.

When I got home from school, I told my dad that I was thinking about joining the national guard. He was surprised that I was even interested in the military. Nothing about it fit my personality or the direction I had been going with my life. We had a brief conversation about it and didn't discuss it again until the recruiter was at our house a few days later.

The recruiter talked with my dad about what I would be going through and what to expect. The meeting was quick since he had been through the same discussion a couple of months earlier regarding my stepsister. My dad asked about past football injuries and my general lack of coordination, thinking it would keep me from getting in. Satisfied with the answers the recruiter gave, my dad signed the parental permission form allowing me to enlist as a minor.

I drove to my mother's house that night to get her permission. She was not as cooperative as my father. She didn't want to let me join because I would end up going to war in Iraq. I tried to bring her to her senses by telling her that there wouldn't be a war in Iraq and that, even if there was, my unit would be safe because we were being deployed to Bosnia after my basic training. After nearly an hour I changed tactics and told her that I would just enlist when I turned eighteen anyway. She signed the paper.

The next day I went to a military entrance processing station (MEPS) to have a doctor poke his finger in my ass, fill out some paperwork, and get sworn in. Everything went smoothly and I was home the following day in time for dinner to announce that I was a member of the United States Army.

"Jesus, I didn't think you'd get in," my dad said when I got home. "We didn't even talk about this."

"Well, it's too late now," I assured him.

Too late indeed, I thought as I assumed the front leaning rest position at Fort Benning, Georgia.

CHAPTER 2:
Deployment

WHEN IT WAS TIME FOR LUNCH on my first day of basic training, my platoon lined up in front of the dining facility door in two single-file lines. The orders of the lines were determined alphabetically by our last names. My last name put me in the front of the second line.

"Listen up privates," Drill Sergeant Orellana, a short, bowlegged Dominican man, commanded in a raspy voice that seemed to incite fear into the toughest basic trainees. "When I tell you to come into the chow hall, I want the private closest to the door to look over his right shoulder and give the order: 'File from the right, column right.' Does everyone understand?"

"Yes drill sergeant!" the platoon shouted collectively.

I stood, waiting in a state of low-grade panic for the drill sergeant to re-emerge from the chow hall. I was the closest private to the door and I did not want to fuck up.

"All right, let's fucking go," said Drill Sergeant Orellana, sticking his head out the door.

"File from the right, column right," my voice squeaked over my left shoulder.

"What the fuck was that? Grow a pair of fucking balls and give the order."

"File from the right, column right!" I shouted with as much conviction as I could muster, again over my left shoulder.

"Well that was better, but you still fucked it up. Try again."

"File from the right, column right!" I yelled even louder over my left shoulder.

Members of Bravo Company getting ready to board the bus and leave Thief River Falls, Minnesota, for Camp Shelby, Mississippi, where we would train for our deployment in Iraq.

"Everyone in this line feel free to thank Private . . ." Orellana paused to look at the name tape on my uniform ". . . Mustard for fucking you. He didn't want to follow the instructions and give the command over his right shoulder, so you will all be eating last for the rest of the week. Abrego, lead these dipshits inside."

Abrego, a private whose last name ensured that he would be at the head of just about every alphabetically organized line on the planet, gave the command over his right shoulder and led his column into the chow hall. I stood next to the door watching the other line file past with twenty-five pissed-off hungry people I didn't know standing behind me.

The weeks peeled off of the calendar as quickly as a tortoise giving a blowjob. About the time I'd finished perfecting my escape plan to go AWOL, I was sent to the hospital when I couldn't catch my breath after a run.

A doctor tested me for asthma and gave me a light-duty profile (a doctor's note saying that I couldn't run). For the next three weeks, I waited for the results of my test. With only two weeks left before graduation, my test results were finally in. The doctor explained to me that I had asthma and asked me if I had known this before enlisting. I said no, but that I was very sick just a couple of weeks before I left for basic and I didn't feel like I made a full recovery.

The doctor told me that she was going to start paperwork to process me out of the military. I protested on the grounds that I only had a week of training left and that graduating was, by far, the quickest way out of Fort Benning.

After nearly twenty minutes of pleading, the doctor reluctantly put away her paperwork. "Fine, I will let you finish. I'll give you an inhaler and if you have any trouble you need to come back and see me." She handed me an inhaler. I was released from my profile and sent back to training.

The next morning we woke up and went for a run. Eagle run is a graduation requirement for infantrymen trained in Fort Benning. It is a five-mile company formation run to be completed in less than forty minutes. I felt out of shape, having not run for three weeks, but was still confident that I could finish it—that is until I started running. Then I realized that I had to shit. The urge to evacuate my bowels hit me the minute we got on the road and I started pumping my legs. I ignored the pressure building in my bowel as best I could, but as the poking of the turtle head against my sphincter became more insistent, I knew that this situation would be difficult to maintain.

I managed to push myself past mile three before it really started to get to me. I thought my ass was going to fall out as the group ran past the "one and half miles to go" sign. Fearing the worst was upon me, I fell out of the formation and stopped running to compose myself.

A drill sergeant from another platoon and a major running at the back of the formation encouraged me to finish. "Keep going," they said. "We're almost done." I started running with them, hoping that my bowel had calmed down. I ran in front of the major and the sergeant for another mile before I couldn't hold it anymore. With a half-mile left in the run, I dropped a three-pound turd in my shorts. Luckily the mesh inside of our shorts trapped the stink bomb, so it didn't roll down my leg, but it began to liquefy from the motion of my running.

"What the hell is that smell?" complained the major.

"I just shit my pants," I said without breaking stride.

"Did he just say . . ."

"Yes, he shit his pants," the drill sergeant explained to the major.

They kept encouraging me to finish the run, though now they ran in front of me talking over their shoulders. I finished the run and was loaded into the back of a pickup truck (for some reason they didn't want me in the cab) and hauled back to the barracks, while the rest of the company heard a speech from the battalion commander.

Later that day, after I'd had a chance to wash my ass, the drill sergeant called me into his office. He told me that I'd shown real strength and determination by finishing that run and that I would make a fine soldier one day. It was the only pat on the back I received during basic training and I got it for shitting myself. Two weeks later I graduated and became an infantryman.

■

For the next year I led an unremarkable life. I worked at the airport in Grand Forks, North Dakota, loading and unloading planes for FedEx, kept dating my high school girlfriend Leah, attended community college but quit halfway through the first semester, and went to drill once a month.

In late March 2005, 2-136 Infantry battalion commander Lieutenant Colonel Gregg Parks showed up at drill and addressed the company. On paper, operational control of our company in Iraq would fall under Parks, a squinty-eyed pussbag who would prove himself so afraid of combat that he would earn the nickname "Spineless Six" ("six" is code for a commander— Alpha Company called its commander "Rainbow Six" because he spoke with an effeminate lisp).

I sat at a table near the back of the group with Staff Sergeant Tim "Nelly" Nelson and Specialist Ben Slater. Standing six feet four inches, Nelly towered over almost every other soldier in the company. He had just arrived in our unit from the U.S. Infantry Old Guard Ceremonial Unit in Washington, D.C.

Although not Polish, Slater had a giant Polack nose. It had gotten that way because it was broken at least four times a year from the regular ass-kickings he received in bar fights. He enlisted just a couple of months after me, we went to basic training together, and he was always a reliable friend.

Bryan "Dunna" McDonough boards a plane in Minneapolis on his way to Mississippi.

We tuned out most of Spineless Six's speech and talked about what an incompetent douchebag he was.

"Within the next six months the Minnesota National Guard is expected to be mobilized in support of Operation Iraqi Freedom," Parks said, grabbing our attention. "What we know right now is that if this happens, the Bearcats (the nickname for the 2-136 Infantry battalion) will part of the group that answers that call."

The company let out a collective groan—most of the people in the room were fresh off of a deployment to Bosnia. I would have been sent to Bosnia, too, but I hadn't finished basic training in time to be part of the deployment.

The tents we lived in for our first two weeks on Camp Shelby, before we moved into barracks for six months.

"I know it's hard and that most of you probably haven't even unpacked your bags from Bosnia yet. I haven't unpacked mine, either. It doesn't sound too sexy right now, but I know that the Barbarians (my company's nickname) will step up and answer the call. And that you guys who just returned from Bosnia will step up and bring your experience with us to Iraq."

We weren't given the exact date that we'd be deployed. Not much happened between when we found out we were going to Iraq and when we were actually deployed. We couldn't start new jobs or make any plans because we knew we'd be leaving at some point in the near future, so we were stuck in a purgatory of waiting. We trudged through each day with no enthusiasm, doing nothing worth discussing. Mostly we kept working at our old jobs and drinking as much alcohol as possible. I don't know about the other guys, but I drank to help me forget that I'd soon be going to Iraq. Finally in September we learned we'd be deploying to Camp Shelby, Mississippi, in early October to begin training for our upcoming tour in Iraq. On October 1, 2005, I reported to my armory to begin my mobilization in support of Operation Iraqi Freedom. After months of denial, I could no longer ignore the fact that I was going to Iraq.

We hung around the Thief River Falls armory for a few days, doing paperwork and making sure everyone was ready for deployment. On October 5, we reported to the armory for the last time.

Our families were there to see us off. We said our last goodbyes and got onto the charter bus that would take us to the Fargo airport. The bus left the armory with people lining the streets all the way through town, waving and cheering to give us a memorable send off.

Our nonstop flight landed in post-Katrina Biloxi, Mississippi. It was nearly midnight, so we were unable to see any of the devastation until we got to Camp Shelby, though it could be argued that Camp Shelby already looked like a disaster site before Katrina hit.

We were herded like cattle from plane to bus, from bus to bus, bus to bus, and finally bus to tent on forward operating base (FOB) Hurricane. The FOB was made up of rows and rows of plywood-floor tents sitting on top of the golf-ball-sized rocks that were used by the military to cover the ground at all bases in Iraq to keep dust down.

The next day we were introduced to the men in our platoon who were brought in from the old Alpha Company in our battalion. The original Alpha had been dissolved when we were restructured for the deployment and the original Charlie Company was renamed "Alpha Company."

"When I got my commission as an armor officer, I said that there is no way I would ever work in an infantry unit," First Lieutenant Wade Blomgren said during his introduction to the platoon. "Apparently I pissed off someone because now I am going to Iraq as a platoon leader in an infantry company."

The second person we met was our platoon sergeant, Sergeant First Class Michael Rogers. "Rog" was a big guy with fiery red hair to match his temper and crooked teeth stained from years of chewing tobacco. Despite his lack of visual appeal, he always showed a genuine concern for every soldier.

A little bit later that day, John Kriesel, a sergeant with a scatological sense of humor, joined our squad. He was the Alpha team leader in 2nd Squad.

Horn was Bravo team leader in 2nd Squad, to which I was assigned. Horn was alright, but he was a used-car salesman in civilian life, and like all good salesmen, he had a tendency to get on our nerves. The first day we were there, Horn discovered that Sergeant John Goldstein had relatives in a German concentration camp during World War II. "Hey man, my grandfather died in a concentration camp," Horn told Goldstein.

"Really? Will you tell me about it?" Goldstein asked, feeling a deep cultural connection with Horn's grandfather. Goldstein, a former marine who everyone called "the Hebrew," or just "the Hebe," was enough of a bullshitter himself to usually catch on when someone was full of shit, but in Horn he had met his match.

"Yeah, he fell out of the guard tower."

CHAPTER 3:
Birthday Party

We spent most of our time in Camp Shelby taking classes that would prove meaningless once we got to Iraq. Take, for example, our land navigation training. Typically we would sit—or rather sleep—through the boring classroom segment of the course. On our twenty-fourth day in Shelby, after a good nap during the classroom portion, we went outside for some hands-on instruction on using a compass. We were informed that our job as infantrymen would depend on our knowing two things: how to shoot a rifle and how to use a compass. In theory, this would be useful training. We learned how to use a compass and a map to shoot an azimuth and figure out exactly which direction we were going at any time. The thing was, we used global positioning systems (GPS) to do all this, rendering the training less than useful during our deployment to Iraq.

After the compass training we took a break for lunch. I had the spaghetti and meat sauce meal, ready to eat (MRE), which was the best MRE because it tasted the least like dog shit. Not that I'd ever eaten dog shit, but if dog shit tastes like it smells, it must taste like a beef enchilada MRE.

Once I finished as much of the MRE as my colon could tolerate, we started the navigation course. On a typical land navigation course, we were given one to two hours to find four to six points on a given map. If a soldier with a compass, map, and a protractor knows what he or she is doing and jogs most of the course, the soldier can finish in half an hour. When Sergeant Horn and I set out, we were given a map, compass, protractor, and a GPS. With the GPS we managed to finish the entire course in thirteen minutes.

This fit right in with the rest of the training that I received at Camp Shelby, since it was ridiculously easy and ultimately proved grossly inadequate and pointless once we were in Iraq. At Camp Shelby we were trained to fight in heavily forested areas, we learned to engage Soviet ground troops, and we learned how to detect a type of improvised explosive device (IED) that would never, ever be used in a real-life situation, none of which proved very helpful once we got in-country. A little counter-insurgency training, on the other hand, might have come in handy. But at that time we weren't fighting an insurgency, according to our secretary of defense, so there was little need for such training.

For me the most challenging part of the entire day was trying to dodge the whitetail deer that tried to trample me to death. I have to give props to the deer for setting up one hell of a good ambush. I was walking behind Sergeant Horn on a narrow trail with thick brush all around. I heard a ruckus behind me and turned to see a deer charging down the trail right at me. I was pretty much trapped, but managed to duck into a hole in the brush. The deer cut off of the trail just before getting to Sergeant Horn and went on its way.

The 26th of October, 2005, which also was the twenty-sixth day of our deployment, happened to be Specialist Joseph Ness' birthday. Ness was in 3rd Squad but bunked in the same part of the building as me, because the area where the rest of 3rd Squad lived was full. He was a goofy-looking dude, a little on the portly side. He resembled the character Rod Farva from the movie *Super Troopers*, but he was one of the nicest guys I met in Camp Shelby.

Nobody knew that it was his birthday until his bunkmate Slater overheard Ness' mother singing him the "Happy Birthday" song over the phone. Slater asked, "Ness, is it really your birthday?"

Ness replied, "Shut up man. Somebody might hear you." Ness knew that if we found out it was his birthday, the rest of his day would be a waking nightmare. Anytime anyone in the army finds out that there is a birthday in the platoon, it becomes a group mission to make the birthday boy or girl feel as much shame and humiliation as possible for the rest of the day.

Once Ness had finished pleading, Slater began yelling that it was Ness' birthday and that everyone should come and wish him a happy birthday.

A furious Ness started denying that it was his birthday, but this turned out to be futile because no one really cared if it was or not. The point was to

Lieutenant Wade Blomgren gets taken down while training for hand-to-hand combat. Most of our training at Camp Shelby ultimately proved pointless because we were training to fight a traditional war rather than an insurgency.

alleviate the intense boredom of life in Camp Shelby by trying to humiliate someone, and for the rest of that day that person was going to be Ness.

Nothing really interesting happened to Ness until we were in the chow hall later that evening. I had gone to eat with Ness and Slater so that I could make sure that I could take part in the Ness humiliation party.

We were just finishing chow when Sergeant First Class Travis Ostrom, the platoon sergeant of 2nd Platoon, walked past our table on his way out of the chow hall. "Sergeant Ostrom," I said, "did you know that today is Ness' birthday?"

This news delighted Ostrom. He wheeled around with a big grin on his face and shouted across the chow hall, "Hey, first sergeant!"

Road marching was one of the few useful things we did. In Iraq we usually walked where we needed to go because the odds of hitting an IED in a humvee were so high.

Sergeant Richard Eggert (we called him "Top") was the company's first sergeant, the man in charge of making sure that the soldiers were taken care of. It was his job to see that the soldiers had good living conditions, were fed three square meals a day, and that their family issues got taken care of. His primary job was to keep morale up, but humiliating people on their birthdays was also his responsibility.

Ness pleaded with Ostrom to stop and to let it go, but since Ostrom had already brought Ness' birthday to Top's attention, all the pleading in the world wouldn't put the toothpaste back in the tube. Top said, "Goddamn it, Ness, how the fuck did you slip past my radar? Show me your ID." He studied the card, returned it to Ness, and said, "Well out-fucking-standing, Ness! It is your birthday. You stay right where you are. I'll be back."

Top turned around and addressed the whole chow hall: "All right, everyone listen up. Today is a very special day. It is Specialist Ness' birthday, so everyone had better give him a big round of applause." Top turned around, gave the hand signal for freeze to Ness, walked up to the serving counter, and started talking to the cooks.

Once the applause died down, Ostrom was back with a small piece of cake and a rolled-up napkin. He set the cake down in front of Ness, who had been put on a diet by his squad leader Sergeant Chris Lemke and was not allowed to actually eat it. Ostrom then took the rolled-up napkin and stuck it into the cake like a candle and lit it on fire. The three of us sang "Happy Birthday" to Ness, pausing to relight the napkin about halfway through. Ness thanked us, blew out the napkin, and ate the cake, but only after Slater and I convinced him that we would do his pushups for him if he got into any trouble over the matter.

A few minutes later Top came back to the table with one of the civilian servers from the kitchen, Miss Dominique. She was a fairly large black woman with one of those smiles that seemed stuck right to her face. When she got over to our table, Top pointed to Ness and told her that he was the birthday boy.

Miss Dominique looked at Ness and started singing "Happy Birthday" to Ness in a very soft, gentle, and beautiful voice. Ness got red in the face while Slater and I laughed so hard we started to get stomach cramps.

After she was through singing, Ness stood up and thanked Miss Dominique, gave her a hug, and sat back down. Once she left, Ness thanked Top and we went back to our barracks.

On our way back Ness demanded that Slater and I give him our birth dates so he would be able to get his revenge on us when the day came. Figuring that it was only fair I agreed to give up my birthday despite Slater refusing to divulge any information whatsoever. I wasn't worried about Ness getting his revenge since I figured he'd forget all about it by January.

CHAPTER 4:
Trick or Treat

ONE OCTOBER MORNING our squad leaders woke us up at the ass crack of dawn and bused us out to rifle range forty-three before the sun was up. They didn't even let us have breakfast. When we arrived at roughly 0600 hours, we had to wait outside the gate for the better part of an hour, which was par for the course since Camp Shelby had what must have been one of the most poorly run rifle ranges in the history of rifle ranges.

Once the range cadre arrived and opened the range, we filed off of the bus. We got into firing orders, and an observer controller (OC) told us to wait in the bleachers off to the side.

We sat and waited for quite a while, until the cadre had its morning coffee and started moving. Around 0830 the first firing order got on line and started shooting. We could have just as well slept in and had breakfast, but that seemed to be the way things were done at the Camp Shelby rifle range. By 1100 the sixth firing order had finished, but a fire broke out in the woods about a mile in front of us. We were in the middle of a terrible drought and hadn't had rain in six weeks, so all rifle ranges had to be shut down. By this time I no longer bothered to get pissed off at the incompetent leadership that would try to cram 1,000 people through the firing range in a single day while a wild fire raged all around it. In fact, I almost admired their consistency. If we couldn't rely on anything else, we could at least count on the fact that the army would fuck up anything that could be fucked up.

For the next two hours we just sat around, took naps, and played cards while helicopters worked to put the fire out. I knew right then that I was in

Someone trying to do the impossible—qualify on the rifle range at Camp Shelby.

for a long day since I was in firing order nineteen and we had only finished six when the fire started. Shooting resumed around 1300, when the fire was no longer threatening anything. It hadn't been put out but it had been contained, at least temporarily.

The cadre somehow managed to get eight more firing orders through before the fire picked up again. When we finally got back on the range and it was my turn to shoot, I went to the ammunition shack, picked up my ammo, went to the control point, and got onto the range. When I got to my position, I set myself up in a foxhole because that was almost always the way the first event was shot in an army rifle qualification. The range safety officer came over to my position and informed me that this range was stupid and things were done backwards around here. So, confused, I crawled out of the foxhole just as a voice came over the loud speaker: "Firers, assume a good prone unsupported position alongside the foxhole."

I set myself up beside my foxhole and got ready to start shooting. The voice clicked back onto the loud speaker: "Firers, rotate your selector lever from safe to semi and watch your lanes." This was the command to start shooting any targets that popped up in your lane.

The first target popped up and, as soon as it did, I fired and it went back down again. Then the second, third, and fourth targets came up and went back down. I had a feeling of excitement as I shot the fifth target and thought to myself, as long as I stay calm I could shoot expert for the first time since basic training. The sixteenth target was a three-hundred-meter target and it was the first one that I missed. When I saw the dirt fly up in front of it and saw the target still standing, I was immediately pissed off. I had to gain my composure back and do it quick, as I only had a few precious seconds between targets to get back on track. I closed my eyes, took a deep breath, and told myself, "Calm the fuck down and hit the next one." I actually said this out loud.

I opened my eyes to see the 150-meter target just locking into place. I was back into my groove and it went down a half-second later. I hit the last three

Engaging in a traditional army circle jerk while we wait to go out on the range and qualify.

targets in the prone and was feeling good about my shooting. All I had to do was hit seventeen out of twenty in the foxhole, which is almost always my strong position because we were allowed to use sandbags to support our rifles.

I set up in the foxhole, loaded my weapon, and started looking for targets when I got the command from the speaker. I missed the second and third targets, hit the fourth but couldn't seem to calm myself down after two misses right off the bat. I hit one more target before my weapon malfunctioned and failed to eject the spent shell casing. I did the SPORTS drill—Slap the magazine up into the magazine well; Pull the bolt carrier back; Observe the chamber to make certain it's cleared; Release the bolt carrier to load another round; Tap the forward assist; Squeeze the trigger. It worked as advertized, but I lost two rounds trying to get the gun working again. I fired a shot once I thought I had fixed the problem. I missed that one, but at least the rifle was working again. I hit the next two targets when my bolt locked into the open position. I looked at the ejection port, thinking my rifle malfunctioned again, only to discover that there were no rounds left in my magazine. I'd shot 8 rounds and lost 2 in the malfunction for a total of 10 rounds. That left me 10 rounds short of the 20 I was supposed to get in my preloaded magazine when I stopped at the ammo shack.

Once everyone finished firing the ten rounds that I didn't get, I climbed out of the foxhole in a rage. I walked up to the tower, muttering obscenities under my breath along the way, ready to join the re-fires in the box of shame, the area where the people who didn't qualify the first time go to learn how to shoot all over again.

When I got to the base of the tower where the scores were read off, I was told that I qualified with the bare minimum, twenty-three out of forty, but I could try again with the correct number of rounds. I decided that I was too frustrated at this point to even think about shooting another score.

Two more firing orders were sent out to finish off the daylight. The chow truck rolled in just as the last soldiers were coming off of the firing line. We ate chow and bullshitted until the sun was gone and it was as dark as it was going to get. We had a night qualification to do before we could go back into the barracks and sleep.

When I ran into Winnie, I was still pretty fired up about what had happened earlier. Winnie seemed to have an uncontrollable fetish for firearms

Sergeant John Kriesel shows his displeasure over wearing his protective mask.

and was a better shot with any rifle at any time than almost all of the riflemen in the entire battalion. In Iraq Lieutenant Blomgren picked Winnie to be part of a sniper team that he put together.

I sat down next to him for a few hours and we passed the time talking about our women back home. He talked about my cousin Amanda and I talked about Leah.

The rest of the evening was fairly uneventful. I fell asleep in line next to Winnie (apparently I could sleep through gunfire, but if someone was snoring too loud in the barracks I'd wake up and couldn't get back to sleep) and woke up about an hour later when it was just about time for us to get on the firing line.

McDonough plays with a toy gun while we are drinking in our barracks on Camp Shelby.

I got up, grabbed my fifteen rounds of ammunition, and went to my firing position. I jumped down into my foxhole and got ready to fire again. I needed to hit seven of fifteen targets at 50 meters to qualify. I shot and hit the first seven targets and then decided to have a little fun by putting my rifle on burst, shooting three rounds at a time. Once the firing was over I got my score of ten at the bottom of the tower and got on the bus. By the time I got to bed, it was somewhere around 0215.

A couple of days later the company went back to the range to fire for our nuclear, biological, and chemical (NBC) qualification with the pro-mask. This involved an order to don our protective mask, followed by a twenty-round rifle qualification. This required us to fire ten rounds at each of the two 50-meter targets, hitting 11 out of the 20.

When my firing order came up I was sent to lane three and told by the soldier coming off the range that the 50-meter left target didn't work properly. When I talked to the range cadre about this, I was told that it was working perfectly fine and to just go shoot.

When I got to my foxhole I knew that all I had to do was get the bad target to fall once and I would qualify. So I decided what I needed to do was to put as many rounds as I possibly could into that target. After the fourth exposure of the broken left target, I was out of ammo and all that I could do was hope that one of the ten bullets I put into it had registered. When everyone else had finished shooting I repositioned myself to shoot my last ten rounds at the other target. I managed a perfect ten for ten on that one, so all I needed was just one on the other target to qualify.

When I got to the tower and heard that I had only shot a ten out of twenty, I got a little mad. I walked up to the staff sergeant who had read the scores to everyone to see if he would let me have a gimmie on the broken target. In a dialect that I'd never heard before, something like a hybrid between southern drawl and extremely stupid, he replied (as best as I could interpret), "They ain't nothin' wrong wit dat targit there on lane three. You musov jus miss da targit. Now go..." The rest of that last sentence was completely beyond what I would ever consider to be the English language and I didn't understand any of it. I think he was describing his favorite shrimp dishes or something.

Frustrated that he didn't believe me and that I couldn't understand what he had told me, I explained to him that it was ludicrous to think that I shot a perfect ten for ten on one target but failed to hit the other target even once. He attempted to tell to me that the target was perfectly fine and started saying something about me being a smartass before I walked away.

Fed up with trying to plead my case, I decided to just look like a retard and shoot again. I got onto the re-fire roster and went up on the firing line. Just as I had done in the night fire, I shot the eleven targets I needed to qualify and then put my rifle on burst and had some fun.

A few days later, on Halloween, we were given our first opportunity to drink alcohol. There was a company-wide money pot for anyone who wanted to have some beer that night. Those of us who wanted some alcohol put five dollars into the beer fund.

We used the money to buy the most beer I had ever seen in one place at one time. I wasn't old enough to consume alcohol legally, but I got just as drunk as everyone else anyway. After about an hour of drinking, Neumiller— the youngest member of our fire team who had to join the military because he'd been busted for something horrible, like burglary or drugs, and had been given the choice between joining the military or spending thirty-seven years in prison—found a Halloween mask sitting on a bunk. It was a generic goblin mask, made of translucent plastic so you could see his face behind it. He put it on and started walking around our barracks trick or treating. He didn't really do that well in the barracks; the only thing he got was a shitty MRE, so he decided to try his luck outside the barracks.

He stepped out of the door and into the area where everyone was drinking, playing cards, and listening to music. First sergeant saw Neumiller and called him over to have a closer look. When Neumiller got over there, Top took out his can of Copenhagen long cut, sprinkled a dip of chewing tobacco into Neumiller's trick-or-treat bag, and said, "There you go. Now don't say I never gave you anything."

Once Top was done with him, Neumiller turned to the commander and said, "Trick or treat, sir." The commander chuckled and told him that he didn't have anything for him, but he could do some pushups if he wanted to. At about that time Top told Neumiller to leave before he had to do any physical training (PT).

After he had made the rounds at the party outside, Neumiller took his mask and bag into 2nd and 3rd Platoons' barracks and made out pretty good. He got a fair amount of candy and a few beers.

We ended the night by drawing on Sergeant Chad Hassel's unconscious face with some face paint and went to bed around 0130. The next day was a new month and we had a four-mile company run at 0600.

CHAPTER 5:
Thanksgiving 2005

W<small>E HAD A FAIRLY LIGHT DAY</small> of training on the day before Thanksgiving, and we got that night off. We'd been studying the different weapon systems that we would use when we were in-country. We'd also had classes on different weapon sights, tripods, first aid, and how to react to chemical attacks. A lot of this training was redundant since we knew most of it backwards, forwards, sideways, and inside out from our infantry training.

Before we were let go for the night, Captain Daniel Murphy, our commander, gave us the standard pre-debauchery speech: "I want all of you to get as falling down, shitty, puking drunk as possible, but stay in the company area when you do it. Watch out for your buddy and make sure he doesn't drink himself to death. If your buddy is having a hard time, you need to bring him to a bathroom to puke, give him some water, and put him to bed where he can pass out. If you go into town this weekend and find yourself a woman, make sure you wrap it up so you don't get a disease. We don't want to send any of you home because you got VD from some prostitute. Just stay safe and protect yourself. Have fun in the next day and a half, be safe, and be back here by 2000 hours on Thursday evening. That is all I have for you right now, so go get some beer and have a good night."

Everyone who wanted a grilled steak on the night before Thanksgiving had pitched in ten dollars, so we had a big pile of steaks to grill. Staff Sergeant Kerry Mandt, who would later earn the distinction of commanding the squad that hit the most IEDs in Iraq, started grilling the steaks right after the brief. I made sure to be the first in the line, after loading up my plate with the potatoes

Captain Daniel Murphy gives a stump speech instruct-
ing us on the proper care of our genitals should we
engage the services of professional escorts.

and beans and grabbing a beer. I got the second steak off of the grill because the guy behind me in line wanted his steak lightly heated and still bleeding. I got my medium rare steak, found an open patch of hill, and sat down. I don't know if the steak really was that good, or if I was just that hungry for decent food after eating the dog shit known as MREs for the past two months, but that steak was one of the best I have ever had before and since.

After I ate my steak, I went into the barracks and played cards for a few hours. I wasn't in the mood to get falling down, shitty, puking drunk, so I didn't drink much for the rest of the night. The card game I was playing was relatively new to me. It was called "whist" and it seemed that the more the people in the platoon drank, especially the Bradley crews, the better they got at the game. I lost the five dollars that I had thrown into the pot for the tournament.

Once we had finished the whist tournament I went into the bathroom to take a leak and found Winnie lying on the floor next to the toilet. After I drained the lizard I got Winnie some water and made him sit up. When he finished puking, he fell back on the floor into a puddle of water he had spilled from the cup I gave him. It was getting fairly cold in the bathroom building and I couldn't leave him there to freeze, even though that is what he kept telling me to do, so I went outside to find someone to help me drag him to bed.

When I walked out the door, I saw Sergeant Logan Wallace lying on his back, talking to his girlfriend on his cell phone while Specialist Adam Seed, who was wearing a black, curly haired, mullet-cut wig, stood over him and tried to mount him sexually. I'm not sure why Seed was doing this, but I figured don't ask, don't tell.

I guess if Seed had to hump someone, Wallace was as good a choice as any. He was the most laidback, goofball non-commissioned officer (NCO) I'd ever known. I met Wallace at my first drill, when I was still in high school. He told the newcomers to our unit about an accident he'd had on a dirt bike that involved him carrying his testicles to the hospital to have them re-attached. When we bought into the story and said, "Oh man, that sucks, dude," he started laughing and called us fucking dumbasses for believing him. Later, during a training exercise where I played a Bosnian civilian and had to pretend to not speak English, Wallace tricked me into speaking English so he could face plant me into the ground and beat the shit out of me. Wallace was as good a choice for Seed to hump as anyone.

Seed could have probably humped just about anyone, though, since most people preferred to keep on his good side. Specialist Adam Seed was absolutely batshit fucking *loco*. A rotund man who stood roughly six feet two inches tall, Seed had the ability to drink like no one I'd ever met. He was also one of the most repulsive men I'd ever met, but at the same time he was also one of the funniest. All in all, Seed was just a fun guy to be around, a northern Minnesotan at his best, even if he did have a tendency to hump your leg like a dog.

I helped Wallace pry Seed off of him, and Wallace asked me what I needed. I explained the situation to him and he stumbled into the bathroom behind me.

I picked Winnie up and got him most of the way to the door by myself when Wallace decided to take over. I couldn't fit through the door with the both of them, so Wallace went through the door with Winnie. When they got about ten feet out of the bathroom, Wallace, who could barely walk on his own, fell down, bringing Winnie to the ground with him. I picked the two of them up and we got Winnie into his bed without another incident.

Once Winnie was passed out in his bunk I went into the other half of our building, which was where I slept. When I walked through the door I saw Neumiller and Specialist John Ecker taking pulls from a bottle of Phillips vodka. A tall, lanky guy, Ecker loved to fuck with people, sort of like Joe Pesci's character in *Goodfellas*, only not psycho (as far as I know, Ecker had yet to stomp a man to death the way Pesci did in the film). We knew we weren't supposed to have any hard alcohol, but we were never told specifically not to drink it, so we figured what the fuck.

By the time everyone was truly and completely lit up, First Lieutenant Blomgren walked into our barracks. He took the vodka bottle and everyone cheered, chanting his name, urging him to take a drink. After a few seconds of cheering, we realized that the lieutenant was not there to party. He demanded to know who brought the bottle and said with a drunken slur, "Whoever owns this vodka, meet me outside in thirty seconds." Not wanting any one person to get into trouble over the deal, we decided that everyone there, including a perfectly sober me, would go outside and accept the punishment as a team.

When the lieutenant heard this, he decided to keep it in the building, so he had us all assume the pushup position. We stayed in this position for about

The infamous Mike Neumiller holds the slightly less infamous bottle of vodka.

four or five minutes while Blomgren talked about what a lenient leader he was and how he didn't want to have to be a dick. Meanwhile, we were getting tired from holding the pushup position and arched our backs to relieve the pressure. Blomgren stopped in mid-lecture and screamed, "Get your fucking backs straight!" While he shrieked, Specialist Corey Rystad, a guy from Red Lake Falls who would be my roommate once we got to Iraq, proceeded to heave his guts all over the floor. The lieutenant saw him puking and said, "Get him out of here."

Once our platoon leader got done yelling at us about the liquor, he left. Everyone in the room started bitching about how fucked up it was

Judging by the grin on his face, Corey Rystad is probably thinking about something that made him happy, like beef jerky.

that Blomgren was in our business. That was a duty reserved for the platoon sergeant, whose primary job was to make sure that his Joes were taken care of.

While most of the people in the barracks were bitching about Blomgren, Sergeant Nelson went over to the building where Sergeant First Class Rogers stayed and told him what had just happened.

Within a few minutes Rogers was somewhere outside in the vicinity of our barracks yelling at the lieutenant. I don't know what he was saying to Blomgren, but he didn't sound the least bit happy with him. Some of us were trying to listen in on the ass chewing. We couldn't make out much, but we were quietly cheering for Rog.

Later that night we heard the slap of a human belly hitting a cement floor. It was Rystad, who'd fallen out of his bunk. Kriesel checked to make sure he was all right and we went back to sleep. After that we called Rystad "Airborne."

This was the first of many incidents in which Rystad would get drunk and fall out of his bunk. In hindsight, it might have behooved him to switch to a bottom bunk.

On Thanksgiving Day, I woke up around 0930. I felt good after sleeping in so late and expected to have my best day yet in Camp Shelby. I was excited because I was finally going to be able to call Leah and was hoping to work out some of the troubles we'd been having. I was looking forward to getting out of the barracks alone for a change. I was getting sick of being thrown together with forty other guys who always smelled like sweaty balls, with only three square feet of personal space that was regularly violated.

I managed to get showered, shaved, and dressed by about 1130. I went to the dayroom to check my email and talk to anyone who might be on instant messenger. After about twenty minutes, Leah signed in.

I texted her for about two hours. I'm not sure how or why it happened, but at the end of our conversation she broke up with me. We were talking about what I wanted to do while I was home for Christmas leave, and then all of a sudden she was saying that she was too young and that she couldn't wait a year and a half for me to come home so we should take a break.

And just like that, two and a half years of a relationship was gone in an instant over the cold, emotionless, and wholly depressing form of communication known as instant messaging.

Once the computer lab in Spain—where Leah was studying abroad—had closed for the night and Leah had to leave, I got off of the computer and walked around post for a while, making a few phone calls to some people I thought I could talk to.

Following my phone conversations I continued to walk around post, gathering my thoughts on the day's events, thinking about what had gone wrong with Leah. I wondered if our relationship was worth trying to fix. I started thinking about what I could do to make things work between us while I was deployed, but came up with a whole lot of not much.

The worst rendition of "Diamonds and Pearls" I have ever heard interrupted my thoughts. I don't know who the soldier was, but he was singing it for the talent show the brigade was putting on as part of the Thanksgiving festivities. I wandered over to the stage and watched the show for about two hours before I got sick of it. I did think that the guy who was singing "Diamonds and Pearls" when I first arrived should have won just for comedic value, but the judges thought otherwise.

By this time it was almost 2100 so I went back to the barracks to sleep. When I got there I spent a good thirty minutes badmouthing Leah with Grub, which I thought would make me feel a little better. And it did, until we stopped and I had to lie down to sleep. I was alone with my thoughts once again. I felt alone with my thoughts for the next few days, even though I was living with forty other men who were quickly becoming brothers to me, sweaty balls and all.

CHAPTER 6:
Felonies and Misdemeanors

S PECIALIST JASON HILLIGOSS had been friends with Grub and me before we'd been deployed. He was from Warroad, Minnesota, about 90 miles from my dad's farm, where he went to high school and was an accomplished track runner. Hilligoss and I both moved to Grand Forks, North Dakota, after high school and Grub moved to Fargo, North Dakota. Every once in a while Grub came up to Grand Forks and we got drunk with Hilligoss. That was pretty much the extent of our friendship with the guy.

One day in early December I was sitting at a table in the chow hall with Sergeant Randy Fish, Sergeant Hassel, Specialist Hilligoss, and Specialist Kliner. We were having a relatively normal meal until Hilligoss asked, "Hey Hassel, do you know how much an ACOG (advanced combat optical gunsight) costs?"

"How the hell would I know how much it cost?" Hassel replied.

"I lost mine in the field while we were on the squad live fire range," he told Hassel. Apparently it had fallen off of his rifle so he had to buy a brand-new one to replace it.

We should have suspected Jason was up to something. He was one hell of a good liar. He could convince people to believe whatever stupid thing he could dream up. Some friends and I once brainstormed a list of adjectives to describe him and came up with the following:

- Childish
- Hick
- Smartass
- Mildly retarded
- Simpleton
- Damaged person
- Butt cowboy

It wasn't the most useful exercise, since Hilligoss really wasn't most of those things, especially a cock smoker, at least as far as we knew. He had earned the "butt cowboy" appellation because of the faggy way he wore his boonie hat. He could be a childish smartass and he most definitely was a damaged person, but that could be said about any of us. We must have just been on the receiving end of one of his practical jokes when we made this list.

Apparently this ACOG nonsense started out as a trick on me. When I got up to refill my glass of fruit punch–flavored Powerade, Hilligoss told the rest of the table that he was trying to screw with me and to just play along. When I sat back down he started talking about the incident in more detail. After listening to this ludicrous story of his for a minute or two, I realized that since this was Hilligoss talking, I was probably being messed with.

By that time, we needed to fuck with each other just to take our minds off the depressing December weather, and the fact that there was absolutely nothing to do at Camp Shelby but take naps or watch movies.

The food didn't help our moods much, either. Take MRE number four: cheese omelet with vegetables. Visually it resembled one of those plastic pads of fake vomit. It was not edible, but it jiggled when it hit the ground, which at least provided some entertainment value. It smelled like shit, as did most MREs. When I first opened one, I thought to myself, *It looks like shit. It smells like shit. I wonder if it tastes like shit.* Sure enough, it tasted an awful lot like shit.

My family situation wasn't helping my state of mind much. After twelve years of marriage, my father had kicked my hideous monstrosity of

We played stick ball to relieve the mind-numbing boredom at Camp Shelby. Here, Ben Slater uses a broomstick to hit a tennis ball.

a stepmother out of the house. This happened the day after I went to basic training and their divorce had gotten ugly—or more accurately, the post-divorce had gotten ugly. After a few months of being divorced, the miserable slop hog decided to get revenge on my father for booting her worthless ass to the curb. Apparently the best revenge she could think of was to have him charged with seven felonies and have him face up to one hundred years in prison. The charges were based on lies and exaggerations, and we had ample evidence to prove she was lying about each and every one of them. But she shopped around until she found a sympathetic prosecutor in a county over one

Dunna, Rystad, Micheletti, and Kriesel sit with Santa Claus
at the mall in Hattiesburg, Mississippi.

hundred miles away (which was how far she had to travel to find a prosecutor who wasn't familiar with her reputation for lies and deceit) and had my father brought up on these bullshit charges.

In all he was charged with seven felonies, two terroristic threats, two attempted assaults with a deadly weapon, and three fifth degree sexual assaults. While I was at Camp Shelby I found out that my father's court date had been pushed back another two months. Eventually, the evil cow's dishonesty became apparent even to the district attorney prosecuting the case, and all the felony charges were dropped (after two years of hell and nearly $100,000 in legal fees), but while I was in Camp Shelby most of the charges were still pending.

Between that, breaking up with Leah, and the generally grim December weather, I felt like I had a little too much on my plate. I knew my strings were wound too tight when Miss Bolton, a lady who worked in the chow hall, asked me how I was doing and I responded: "Well ma'am, my girlfriend just left me, my family doesn't understand why I am here, my body aches, the food sucks, and I have a rash on my ass. But otherwise I can't complain."

At least Christmas was coming and I was excited to get out of the little corner of hell known as Camp Shelby, Mississippi. But the POGs even tried to fuck up Christmas for us.

In the military, POG (pronounced *pogue*) stands for "people other than grunts." The basic qualifications needed to be a POG are:

- Have a cushy job such as "personal finance"
- Possess gross ineptitude in the basic skills needed to survive in combat
- Possess gross ineptitude in the basic skills needed to function in a cushy POG job
- Have a general disregard for the grunts who will save a POG's inept ass if a POG ever gets into any kind of fight

POGs will always fuck grunts in the ass if given a chance. They will do anything and everything in their power to make the lives of the grunts a living hell. Grunts can never trust or befriend POGs under any circumstances because they will: (a) be disowned by their fellow grunts and (b) get fucked in the ass by the POGs at the first opportunity.

POGs are a necessary evil in the bureaucracy that is the U.S. Army; they're needed to deal with travel plans and bus scheduling and other logistical crap like that, but they should be avoided at all costs.

Most of the POGs in our brigade were from the southern half of Minnesota, primarily from the Minneapolis–St. Paul metro area. The day that the bus roster for Christmas leave came out, we saw that the departure time for the bus going to Minneapolis was 1400 on December 21 and the Thief River Falls bus was leaving at 1930 on the same day. Thief River is roughly a six-hour drive north of Minneapolis. The buses going north of Minneapolis from Mississippi would most likely pass through the metro area on their way up.

So we had two buses traveling in the same direction at the same speed with the same scheduled stops. One bus was leaving five and a half hours earlier than the other. The bus that was leaving later would drive roughly six hours farther north than the early bus. How much later would the second bus arrive at its final destination than the first? Hint: If the first bus left second and the second bus left first, they would reach their destination at roughly the same time.

In other words, the bus going north, where I was heading, would arrive twelve hours later than the bus carrying the POGs to Minneapolis. This was a classic example of a POG fucking a grunt. I would be screwed out of twelve hours of leave because some POG wanted to see his sperm-bag of a girlfriend six hours earlier.

I looked at the roster and decided then and there that I would have my revenge. I planned to work out my anger issues on the POGs for messing with my scheduled leave by raining down upon them with a hellfire so sadistic that they would pray for a death that would not come quickly enough.

Then, at the last minute, someone in charge realized how completely screwed up this scheduling was and reversed the schedule, so I didn't have to get medieval on POG asses with a blowtorch and a pair of pliers. I would have to find another hobby while finishing out my time at Camp Shelby.

CHAPTER 7:
GP Large Disaster

ONE MORNING IN THE MIDDLE OF JANUARY 2006, I awoke to the sound of roaring wind, flapping canvas, and various curses being shouted by the other members of my squad. We were on a practice mission, guarding a radio relay point near training FOB Hurricane. When I poked my head out of my sleeping bag to see what was causing the ruckus, I saw that a large gust of wind had knocked over our general purpose (GP) large army tent. Madness surrounded me.

Second Squad had been tasked out to a radio relay point to perform security operations. When we arrived shortly after nightfall on a calm January night, there was a GP large tent (roughly sixty feet long and twenty feet wide) set up on a plywood floor to shelter us from the rain that would come in the early morning.

Grub, Horn, and I took the first shift while the rest of the squad slept. We rotated shifts throughout the next 24 hours, having 3 hours on and 6 off. After our first completely uneventful three hours we went into the tent to get some much-needed sleep.

Six hours later, it was again our turn to pull guard duty. At 0700, after another calm three hours, we went back into the tent for more sleep. We'd been running missions for almost forty-eight hours and were tired. I fell into an almost instant deep sleep when I laid down on my cot. Just thirty minutes later I awoke to Specialist Bryan "Dunna" McDonough—a guy from Maplewood, Minnesota, who had joined our squad a month earlier—shouting, "Oh shit! It's coming down." When I pulled the sleeping bag off my

McDonough and Slater hanging out in a tent.

face, I watched the back of the tent become the front of the tent, up become down, and serenity turn into mayhem. As I watched the massive tent buckle and strain under the weight of the storm, I tried to formulate a plan of escape. The main thrust of my still-forming plan was to avoid being injured by the inevitable collapse of our tent.

When the smaller six-foot tent poles started to fall one at a time, I realized that my time for planning had run out. I watched the smaller poles fall to the ground, the ropes snap, and the sides of the tent flare up, revealing the terrible weather outside. Once the sides of the tent started to flap wildly and the wind got underneath the roof, the large twenty-foot tent poles started to fall down. At this point, I took cover. I rolled off my cot, still mostly inside of my sleeping bag, and rolled underneath the cot, hoping it would take the brunt of any falling pole and keep it from crushing me.

When everything had settled into a large pile of canvas, wooden poles, and military gear, I crawled out from underneath the clusterfuck pile to have a look at the carnage. By then it had started to pour and the wind blew with insane force. Most of the area that was originally covered by the tent was now exposed and beginning to soak up the downpour. The rest of the tent was the area where half of the squad had been sleeping, and they were now trapped by the wet, heavy canvas. We tried our best to free the trapped soldiers and cover up our soaking shit.

Shortly after everything came crashing down the rain stopped, the wind died, and the sun came out. The squad worked hard for about two hours to

Me surveying the wreckage, wearing only my drawers. I was happy that I didn't have morning wood.

A week after the tent collapse, the entire brigade was on the parade field to pose for a triumphant photo for Colonel David Elicerio, or "the Elicerio," as he referred to himself. I am in the top of the skull with my middle finger in the air. *Minnesota National Guard*

repair the tent and get all of our gear dry. By the time we had accomplished this, I was too worked up to go back to sleep. Just as I started to relax, chaos and anarchy returned for round two.

The next wave of the storm started off in an all-of-a-sudden sort of way. Everyone looked at the poles along the southern wall of the tent when we first heard the canvas rustling in the wind. Everything looked as if it was going to hold up. We had spent the better part of the morning replacing all of the stakes with longer ones and then tightening the ropes, so we were fairly confident that the tent would hold up this time. After the initial shock of the wind picking back up had passed, I relaxed again.

Not more than five minutes later, the first rope snapped and all hell began to break loose. The side poles began to lift up off the ground, the walls of the tent began to flap wildly, and the center pole I had been leaning on gave way.

After the large center pole slid out of place, the wind got underneath the tent and the whole thing became one massive parachute. Once the tent started to lift off, ropes snapped left and right. I grabbed one of them, hoping to hold up the tent long enough for the others to get out. This proved to be an extremely difficult task.

I managed to hold up the massive pavilion for a few minutes, but no one in my squad left the tent because they were trying to hold the thing up from the inside. When it started to go down, everything collapsed on top of a few lumps trying to tunnel their way out. There was also a large pole that had punctured the canvas and was now proudly enjoying its freedom outside the tent.

In less than three minutes the work that had consumed our entire morning had been reduced to a wet pile of ripped canvas, broken rope, and shattered wooden poles. We decided that the wind gods didn't want us to have a tent anymore. We spent the rest of our time at the radio relay point sleeping under a makeshift lean-to.

CHAPTER 8:
Fort Polk

IN EARLY FEBRUARY THE BRIGADE MOVED from Camp Shelby, Mississippi, to Fort Polk, Louisiana. I couldn't imagine that there was a worse military installation than Camp Shelby anywhere in the contiguous United States until I saw the Joint Readiness Training Center (JRTC) area of Fort Polk, where troops went to train for deployment to Iraq.

The charter bus dropped us off in front of a large building that looked like a huge garage. This was in fact what it was, but instead of housing vehicles it was a cheap way for the army to cram a few hundred soldiers into a small area.

The miserable living conditions offered zero privacy, making masturbation nearly impossible. This caused a lot of tension within the company.

We were in Fort Polk to conduct a two-week mock war in a heavily wooded area, and the February temperature was a chilly fifty degrees. This made complete sense because everyone knew we'd be fighting in the cool, heavily wooded areas of Iraq. It was an extremely useful training exercise.

We moved out to a place called FOB Comfort (similar to FOB Hurricane on Camp Shelby) that was anything but comfortable. The walk to the shower was about five hundred meters, taking us past the chow hall that served meals that were substandard even for the military. Our sleeping arrangements consisted of cramped rows of cots set up in the converted garage.

We started training the day after we got to FOB Comfort. We conducted a practice humanitarian mission of some kind, but that faux mission went

Slater's frustration manifested itself through flamboyance.

completely off the rails when we had to save the brigade's field artillery unit from total destruction.

The 1-125 field artillery unit was sent to raid a village almost daily for reasons comprehensible only to the inscrutable mind of our great-and-all-powerful brigade commander, Colonel David Elicerio—or "the Elicerio," as he referred to himself. And nearly every time they did so, they would have 40 to 70 percent of their force killed in action by the time we arrived. A sane commander might have contemplated sending the mechanized infantry company to do the work instead of the field artillery, but then again sane commanders generally don't refer to themselves in the third person. The thought of sending in the mechanized infantry never seemed to have crossed the Elicerio's mind.

After a week of running around Fort Polk bailing other units out of trouble, we were told that we would be doing our own missions and that we were done helping the 1-125. I was naïve enough to believe this, so when we were told we were to go on a two-hour humanitarian mission to bring school supplies and water to a small village, I packed for a two-hour humanitarian mission to bring school supplies and water to a small village.

Before the mission we practiced Bradley fire drills in the motor pool, because a few days earlier one of the Bradleys we drew from Fort Polk caught on fire. During the fire drill I rolled my ankle. The medic wrapped it up with an ace bandage and we continued with the mission.

One and a half hours into our two-hour mission we got a call saying that B Battery of 1-125 was getting its ass kicked again and was down to just one platoon. Pissed off that we had once again been burned by the Elicerio's water-headed plan to turn the artillery battalion into an infantillery battalion, we drove to the village to deal with the problem.

When we got there we dismounted and prepared to assault. We sat in a ditch and waited for the rest of the platoon to get into position. We were approached by an observer controller. "What are you going to do next, sergeant?" the army captain asked Horn.

"Well sir, I am going to take my team to clear that building and put my machine gunner on the roof to set up a support-by-fire position for the whole village," Horn replied, displaying an unusual flash of military genius.

"Brilliant!" the captain shouted, slapping Horn on the back before running back into the woods.

We waited for another couple of minutes until the others were in place and we did just as Horn told the captain we would. Once the village was secure we got ready to go back to base. With my ankle now the size of a grapefruit, I was looking forward to the end of our now six-hour mission.

Just before we were going to take off, we got a call on the radio telling us that we needed to stay in the village for twenty-four hours to keep a security presence. The butt-fucking we were encountering cemented our already bitter contempt for our battalion and brigade command.

Once the infantillery was gone we tried to raise our morale by playing with the small herd of goats that wandered around the area. Staff Sergeant Todd "Eve" Everson and Specialist Gib Trontvet spent the day luring one of the goats

The Elicerio, doing his impersonation of a walking erection. *Minnesota National Guard*

into the back of their Bradley. Trontvet and Eve never told us why they were trying to catch the goat, but we had our suspicions.

When we got back to our humvee, Kriesel made jokes about me being a hoofed animal. He gave me the nickname "Pan" and joked that I should go hang out with my goat cousins. Figuring that there is no way to beat Kriesel, I decided to go along with him. I got out of the truck and started feeding the goats, cracking jokes about one of "my cousins" having a really nice ass.

Nelly began to have trouble with Kowalenko in the next humvee over. Specialist Jermaine Kowalenko was our platoon's only black guy, earning him the unimaginative nickname "Token." He was having an attitude problem because he didn't want to wear his goggles. Nelly was yelling at him and putting Token's goggles on for him.

"That's assault!" Token said, pushing Nelly.

Horn, who had come over to assist in the attitude adjustment, grabbed Nelly before he could deliver the ass-whooping Token deserved. Eventually they got Token to wear the goggles, but it took a lot of yelling and arguing.

Some goats run to my humvee for protection after escaping from unspeakable depravity inside Staff Sergeant Todd "Eve" Everson's Bradley.

We took turns manning the machine gun and sleeping throughout the night. The next morning, we started to return to base. But on our way back, in hour thirty of our two-hour mission, we got another call saying that we needed to continue from the mission we had just left to begin that day's new mission.

Our bitter contempt for our command turned into seething rage as we went onto that day's mission, a twenty-four-hour detail guarding an electrical

67

power plant. Our commanders did us a favor by relieving us two hours early. At the fifty-two-hour mark, we finally made it back to base.

■

When our two weeks in the field were over, we took all of our vehicles to the wash rack to clean them for turn-in to Fort Polk. The wash rack was a giant outdoor carwash. A crew of ten guys aimed high-powered water spigots at the vehicles as they were driven through.

We had this detail for three days and spent most of it trying to figure out how to soak the guys driving the vehicles. We also spent a lot of time spraying each other, doing our best to knock each other over with the powerful water spray.

Sergeant Randy Fish didn't think it was nearly as entertaining as we found it. After he threatened us with punishment if we didn't stop, we waited for our chance to fuck with him. We struck when he announced that he was going to take a shit and that we had better not be spraying each other when he came out.

When he entered the portable toilet—everyone called them "porta-shitters"—a couple of us ran over. I held the door shut while Specialist Oleg Yagudayev—an Uzbek immigrant who we called "Yogi"—and Specialist Paul Thorn, a fister (fire-support specialist) assigned to our platoon, moved another porta-shitter in front of the door so that he couldn't get out. We left him inside the putrid shit receptacle for about ten minutes before we sent someone over to let him out, knowing that whoever went would be blamed for the entrapment.

Fish wigged out when he came out of the port-a-shitter, yelling at everyone and trying to make us do pushups. No one did any pushups because no one respected him, which made him yell that much louder. Finally either his throat got sore or he realized he wasn't going to get anywhere and decided to say, "Fuck it." He shut up and left us to continue our tomfoolery.

After that we had three days of doing nothing before we were scheduled to leave Fort Polk. We didn't work, we didn't go out, we didn't train. We just hung around our garage barracks watching movies, playing video games, and beating off when a rare moment of privacy presented itself.

Before we could become overwhelmed by our busy schedule, we left Fort Polk. We loaded onto a charter bus and got situated for the six-hour ride. Just before we started moving, the driver stood up to say a few things to us.

"I just want to go over a few things before we leave," the fat old man said in his thick southern drawl. "Please respect my bus and keep it clean and don't write on the seats. If you use the bathroom, please make sure that you get everything inside of the toilet. I don't really like cleaning up in there after y'all make a mess.

"The last thing I want to talk about is respect for the driver. Now I'm a Christian man and I don't need to be hearing all of these curse words. I don't want to hear any of this motherfuckin' or Goddamnin' on this bus. So if you could just keep that to yourselves, that would be great."

The man shut up and started to drive the bus. Pissed off that we were being censored by the bus driver, we collectively decided to put the movie *Waiting* into the bus' DVD player. The movie lasted only a few minutes before one of the waitresses started bitching about something and said "fuck" eight times in two minutes. Most of the guys told the driver to have a nice motherfucking day when we got off of the bus back at Camp Shelby.

Micheletti feels the full force from the powerful spray of two men.

CHAPTER 9:
Welcome to Camp Fallujah

D URING THE TWO REMAINING WEEKS at Camp Shelby, the commander let us drink a lot more often. With not much training left to do, we filled our time with more and more excessive pranks.

For instance, one morning Goldstein put some pubic hairs into Rystad's coffee. Rystad unknowingly drank the coffee and complained that there was hair in it. When Goldstein laughed at him and told him that the hairs were his pubes, Rystad kept his cool. He calmly told the Hebrew to fuck off and began plotting his revenge.

A few days later, Corey found Goldstein's toothbrush unattended. With Kriesel videotaping the event, Corey shoved the toothbrush up his ass. The next day after Goldstein finished brushing his teeth, Corey showed him the video, and Goldstein got another toothbrush and re-cleaned his mouth. A pattern of escalation had begun.

A few days later, Jimmy went home for his grandfather's funeral. When he left, he gave his locker key to Jones in case anyone needed to get into his locker. The day before Jimmy came back to Camp Shelby, Jones and Goldstein emptied out his locker, packed all of his stuff into boxes and duffle bags, and set them on his bed.

The company was drinking the night he returned. When Jones picked Jimmy up at the airport he called back to camp to let everyone get ready.

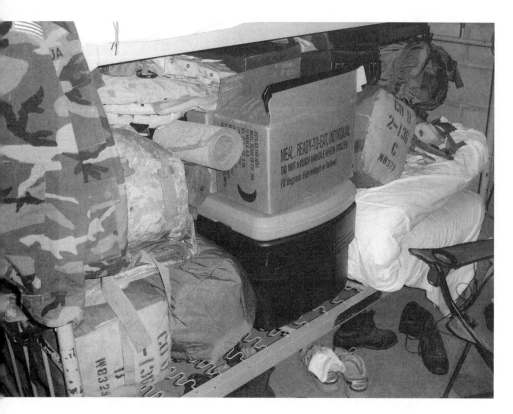

A clever prank.

Dunna set up a hidden camera to capture the moment, while other people gathered to welcome him back.

"What the fuck is this?" Jimmy asked, pissed that all of his shit was out on his bunk.

"Well, I have some bad news for you, Jimmy," Jones explained. "While you were gone you missed some training, and because of that you were moved to headquarters platoon for the deployment. They are replacing you with a guy who did all of the training."

"That's so fucked up! I am going to go talk to the first sergeant right fucking now. I can't believe you didn't stand up for me. What the fuck?" Jimmy stormed out of the building. He was so mad that he didn't even hear everyone laughing at him.

Jones chased him out of the building and stopped him from waking up the first sergeant. When they finally calmed him down enough, they told him that they were fucking with him.

He went back into the building laughing with everyone else. Then he realized that he had to get all of his shit put away before he went to bed. "You assholes! I have to put all of this shit away now."

A bit later that night Rystad wandered away from the group, saying that he had to piss and that he'd be right back. When he didn't return after half an hour, Everson decided to go look for him. When Eve entered the latrine, steam was billowing out of the showers.

Worrying about Corey's safety, he went in to check on him. When he looked into the running shower stall, he saw Corey sitting on the filthy bench in the shower, buck naked, engaged in an act resembling autoerotic stimulation. Eve couldn't believe his eyes—after leaving in disgust, he went in for another look. Sure enough, there was Rystad sitting on the bench stroking his salami.

Everson left without being detected by Corey but then ran into Gallagher, who was coming into the bathroom. "Hey, go check out what is in that shower," he told Gallagher. Gallagher took a look and the two of them rushed back to the barracks to tell the rest of us about Corey's self abuse on the shower bench.

It wasn't Corey jerking off that grossed us out; we all whacked off at Camp Shelby every spare moment we got—we had to, or our balls would have exploded. We were disgusted because he was jerking off while sitting on that slime-covered bench, which was generally the aiming point for our splooge stream when we jerked off. He was sitting in the ejaculate of 150 other men while he jacked off. I wouldn't have sat on that bench with Myrold's ass.

A few days later, the send-off celebration began. Our families came to Camp Shelby to see us one last time before we shipped out to the Middle East for a year.

On the first day of the celebration the Elicerio had his big, proud ceremony. He gave a long-winded bullshit speech about the Red Bulls being the greatest fighting force since Genghis Khan's Mongol hordes defeated the Tanguts in 1227 and how he was more powerful than God almighty and Bill Gates combined and how his farts smelled like Glade daisy-scented plug-in air fresheners, or something like that, but I wasn't really paying very close

75

Rystad with his parents Jim and Donna in Mississippi.

attention. I remember him saying: "I'll be leading the way into Iraq and I'll be covering your rear on the way out." This would be the last time we would see him for eight months.

After the Elicerio's speech, a few other people gave bullshit speeches about the Red Bulls all having foot-long trouser snakes and titanium balls. Then to wrap up the ceremony Tim Pawlenty, the governor of Minnesota, gave a speech about how proud the state was that we had answered the call to war. This bullshit speech upset me. Truth was, Pawlenty had answered the call for us and hadn't given us much choice in the matter.

To finish the pompous charade, the entire brigade paraded past the Elicerio and all of our families. It was strikingly similar to the videos of the Nazi troops marching past Hitler. The difference was that we weren't fascists and we really didn't give a fuck about our commander, the El Douchebag.

The next few days we just hung out and literally drank a truckload of Grain Belt Premium beer. Grain Belt, which brews its beer in Minneapolis,

Minnesota, sent a truckload of beer to Mississippi for us to enjoy before we left the country.

After all of the bullshit ceremonies and mandatory fun ended, we were given a four-day pass. I said goodbye to my parents and drove to Panama City Beach, Florida, with Leah. We'd patched things up while I was home over Christmas. After our vacation to Florida, we were sure we would make it through the deployment, but we broke up again within three months.

In Florida we did some sightseeing and some swimming in the Gulf of Mexico, but mostly we just stayed in the hotel room and did it like rabbits. One night we walked down a pier and talked. On our way off of the pier, we met a man stumbling to the end. When we got off of the pier we heard a splash. I ran to the end of the pier and found the man in the water hanging onto a pillar

The Elicerio in a humvee during the pass and review. He promised to be the first one into Iraq and the last one to leave, then drove off of the parade field and was not seen by anyone in Bravo Company for eight months. *Minnesota National Guard*

Second Squad, First Platoon, group photo an hour before we left Kuwait for Iraq.

and yelling for help. He'd stripped down to his tighty whities and had left his clothes in a pile on the pier. "Are you going to be okay?" I shouted to the man. "Can you swim to me?"

"Where are they?" the man shouted back. "I can't find them! We have to get the fuck out of here!"

I dug around in his clothes and found his wallet. In his wallet I found a military ID. Leah kept trying to talk to him while I called the police. He didn't seem to notice us and continued yelling and swearing at his nonexistent army buddies.

Just before the cops showed up, one of his buddies arrived and explained that he had gone through some rough shit in Iraq and had just gotten back. They dragged him out of the water and Leah and I went on our way. This did not seem like a good omen for my upcoming deployment to Iraq.

78

The C-130 that carried us into Iraq.

The last day in Panama City Beach I drove Leah to the airport. I parked in front of the terminal and got out of the car to say goodbye. She cried on my shoulder for a minute before we were hassled by a cop.

"Sir! Sir! You can't park there, sir! You need to move your car immediately, sir!" shouted a thick-mustached policewoman.

"Okay ma'am, I'll move it in just a minute. I'm about to go to Iraq and would like just another minute to say goodbye to my girlfriend."

"All right, you have one minute."

I continued my goodbye and was interrupted just before Leah was going to leave to fly home.

"Sir, I timed you and was nice enough to give you an extra half minute. You need to move your car immediately."

"Look lady, I don't know what your problem is. I am just trying to say goodbye to my girlfriend before I go to war. I know you and your mustache probably can't comprehend what that means, but there are no other cars in the loading zone and I hardly think that I am a security threat, so would you just back the fuck off and let me say goodbye!"

After finally finishing off my goodbye to Leah, I went back to my hotel room and got drunk before going back to Camp Shelby the next day.

79

The accommodations on the C-130 make flying coach on a commercial airline look downright luxurious.

Kriesel standing by the Camp Fallujah sign.

On March 27, 2006, a couple days after our pass ended, we woke up at the ass crack of dawn and loaded onto a bus headed back to Biloxi, Mississippi. There we loaded on the airplane that would fly us to Kuwait. After an amount of time that seemed impossible to track and included a layover in Bangor, Maine, and Shannon, Ireland, we landed in the Kuwait heat.

We moved into a tent city in Camp Beuhring and did some pointless training for about a week and a half. The training was only superior to what we received in Camp Shelby because we were doing it in a desert.

On the last day in Kuwait, Horn ran into a woman in the gym who we knew from our time at Fort Polk. She worked with us to help search female Iraqis during our training. She told Horn that she wanted to do me before we left Kuwait, which we would be doing in just a few hours. When Horn got back to the tent, he threw me a condom and told me to go find her

Ron Burgundy gives advice to the struggling country of Iraq.

before we had to leave. I had three hours to find her, get laid, and get back in time to fly into Iraq.

I searched every place I could think of on the base but was unable to find her. The only explanation I could come up with was that she wanted me so bad she was doing the same thing and looking in every place I was just behind me. Of course either her or Horn could have been pulling my leg, but I preferred to think she really did want to fuck me bow-legged. I walked back into the tent and disappointed everyone by not having a good sex story to tell them. Two hours later we were on a bus heading back to the airport.

We loaded onto a C-130, squished in like sardines, and took off. The person across the aisle had his knee in the crotch of the guy in front of him. We landed at Camp Taqaddum (TQ), Iraq. We waited there for four days to

Dunna bored out of his skull in a guard tower.

get a helicopter into Camp Fallujah. While we waited our tent collapsed in a windstorm, just like it had in Camp Shelby.

The next day we were playing cards when a few mortars landed near the tent city. We briefly looked up from our card game before we shrugged it off, already complacent from our training in Camp Shelby. Jimmy was only a few meters away from one of the mortars when it landed and was lucky to be alive. The first war stories of the deployment were told that night.

The next night we took a CH-46 helicopter to Camp Fallujah. Most of our battalion had been assigned to TQ because the Marine Corps wanted our Bradleys in Anbar Province, which was under its charge, but Bravo Company went to Camp Fallujah because the marines needed us to do force protection there. Everyone considered Camp Fallujah a shit mission consisting of hour upon boring hour of sitting in towers, so Parks assigned it to Bravo Company because we were the bastard children of the battalion. Parks told us we were going to Camp Fallujah because we were the best, which we knew to be the case, but we also knew he was full of shit. He assigned Alpha Company the job of patrolling the main supply route and keeping it clear for convoys, which everyone expected to be a much more exciting assignment.

We moved into a temporary tent in the south end of camp and went to sleep. The next morning we woke up to see that the tent across from us had been completely destroyed a week earlier by a mortar. A few yards away stood the south entrance to camp, beside a sign that said "Welcome to Camp Fallujah."

CHAPTER 10:
Jameed

I N THE SPRING OF 2006 WE WENT OUT on our first mission in Iraq, a two-week detail guarding a water pumping station called Pump House Barney. Horn, Nelly, and Dunna went out there first to learn how things ran, so they were already there when I got there. A few of the marines who we were replacing briefed us in the morning before Grub, Kriesel, Neumiller, Yogi, Token, Corey, and I left to join the rest of our squad at Barney.

"The IED threat is huge out there," a naval corpsman (medic) briefed us. All the medics with the marines in Camp Fallujah were naval corpsmen and several had been assigned to our company. "You never know when you will hit one. Also, make sure you don't leave the roads because there are sinkholes everywhere. If you hit one of those, you will overturn the truck and kill a bunch of soldiers and marines." The corpsman continued to escalate his lecture until it turned into a tirade about how we were about to enter the trenches of World War III and were all going to die before sunset.

He continued his shrill prognostications about our impending deaths for about ten minutes. It must have been an attempt to frighten us, because the things he was telling us became increasingly more irrelevant. He went from sinkholes and roving bands of thugs, to something that might either have been space aliens or perhaps genetically reconstituted dinosaurs, though by that time he had become so agitated that it was hard to make out what he was saying.

After the brief we loaded ourselves and our gear in a seven-ton truck and left base. We drove down the highway, giving me my first view of the Iraqi desert. It was not nearly what I expected. There were no rolling sand dunes or camels. It looked like a huge gravel pit. The land was wide open and flat with a few piles of gravel scattered around and small, sickly shrubs growing in patches. It looked like North Dakota in the winter, only tan instead of white.

When the convoy got closer to the canal system, I was shocked to see wheat fields. It was mid April and the wheat crop was almost ready to harvest. It reminded me of the home I had already been away from for seven months.

When our truck pulled into the compound, we started unloading the supplies. "Welcome to the suck!" Horn shouted from below the ladder I was standing on while handing down supplies to him from the truck. A few days earlier we'd watched *Jarhead*, a movie about the marines in the first Gulf War, and it seemed that Horn just couldn't help himself.

"Horn, you're a fag," I replied, crushing his self esteem. Once he was sufficiently beaten down, I handed him an air conditioner to replace the broken one that was supposed to cool the room in which I was to stay with the lower enlisted guys.

There were two big buildings in Pump House Barney, one that housed the pumps and one that we used as a barracks. The marines had built guard towers up on the roof of each building. We spent the next couple of days sitting in the towers for twice daily four-hour shifts, playing cards, and avoiding the creepy Iraqi army soldiers who were stationed there with us. The Iraqis were not completely avoidable. In one of the two towers, there was always an Iraqi soldier.

It was only mildly awkward spending four hours in a small area with a man who didn't speak the same language, and I really didn't mind being stationed with the Iraqis. Then I met Jameed. He was the dirtiest of all the Iraqis with us at the pump house, a major accomplishment given how filthy the rest of the Iraqis were, and he always stood entirely too close to me. Iraqis from the major metropolitan areas like Baghdad were generally pretty clean and didn't smell any worse than the rest of us. Most of our 'terps were from Baghdad.

Iraqis from rural areas were a different story. They were old school when it came to personal hygiene and still adhered to the practice of wiping their asses with their left hands instead of toilet paper. As a result, they always reeked of feces. Jameed smelled like a beef enchilada MRE that had been sitting open for a couple of days, so he must have been from a rural area.

Jameed (left) enjoys a cup of chai while he waits for his anti-psychotic drugs to kick in before a tower shift.

I was in the tower with Jameed one day while Rystad and Dunna were in the other tower, happy to be away from him. After nearly thirty minutes of silence, Jameed took it upon himself to spark a conversation.

"Madam?" Jameed asked. I realized he meant "wife" or "girlfriend."

"No madam. You madam?" I replied.

"Two madam," he said, holding up his fingers.

"Wow."

"Baby?" he asked.

"No, no baby. You baby?"

"Yes," he said, once again holding up two fingers.

"Cool. How old?" I asked. He didn't understand, so with a series of grunts and hand gestures I finally managed to convey my question to him. He held up one hand with three fingers and another with five fingers.

"Suck dick?"

"What?" I was sure that he couldn't possibly have asked what I just thought I heard him ask.

"Suck dick?" he asked again, adding a grotesque hand gesture near his mouth so I couldn't possibly misunderstand his question.

"*No!*"

"It's good." He shrugged his shoulders as if to say, *Come on, why not?*

"No, it's not good," I said backing away, now mildly afraid of being anally raped by this heavily armed pervert.

In an attempt to change my mind, Jameed dug his cell phone out of his pocket and began playing a video on it. He beckoned me over to his side of the tower. I didn't want to get too close to the sleazebag, but I could hear the sound of a woman having sex coming from the phone and it piqued my curiosity. Nothing in the extensive catalog of fetish porn that was circulating in the platoon prepared me for what I saw on that tiny screen.

The woman was bent over a table while a donkey stood over her, doing her donkey style with his humongous donkey cock, which was about the size of my forearm. It wasn't quite as gut-churning as the notorious viral video *2 Girls 1 Cup*, but it was in the general ballpark. The next video he showed me involved a woman—not necessarily the same one, though I couldn't be certain because she might just have looked different without a donkey cock up her ass—having sex with and then blowing a black lab.

When the black lab was getting the blowjob, Jameed pointed to the screen and once again suggested, "Suck dick?" I told him to get out of the tower and we spent the rest of the afternoon not speaking.

The next day it was Rystad's turn to be in the tower with Jameed while Dunna and I hung out in the other tower. After an hour on shift, Corey was sitting outside of his tower and looked unhappy.

"What are you doing outside of the tower, Rystad?" Dunna asked over the squad radio.

"That guy kept asking me to suck his dick and then he started watching porn on his phone and beating off in the corner. Then I came out here and he keeps coming out trying to get me to take some pills."

90

"Pills! Fuck, man, send him over here."

"All right. Anything to get him out of here."

When Jameed got to our tower, Dunna asked him about the pills.

"*Hashisha!*" Jameed said with excitement and pulled out a matchbox full of pills. He handed one of the pills to Dunna and swallowed one himself.

"I don't know about this. Should I take it?" Dunna asked me.

"Well, he took one so it isn't going to kill you, and I'm up here with you so if it fucks you up I'll make sure you're okay."

He took it and Jameed looked annoyed.

"Dude, you have to give him something in return for the pill," I explained to him. "He gave you something and in their culture he expects you to give him something in return or he'll be insulted."

"Really?"

"Yeah, dude. Didn't you pay attention in the culture class in Shelby?"

"No."

"Don't feel bad," I said. "I think I fell asleep right after they told us about the gifting customs."

"Okay. What should I give him?"

"He likes blowjobs," I suggested.

"Oh, hell no!" He raised his fists and danced like a boxer. "I should give you the mother of all punches and the two-step shuffle just for saying that. Seriously, what should I give him?"

"I don't know. What do you have?"

"Three dollars," he said and handed Jameed the cash.

Jameed examined it, grunted, and pointed to his hand demanding more cash.

"No, that's all you get," Dunna told him, pissed off that the guy didn't like what he had gotten in return.

We joked with Jameed for another half hour before Dunna said that the pill wasn't doing anything. I loaned him twenty dollars and he bartered for five more. This set the price of the mystery pills for the rest of us. Dunna took two more and kept the rest for later.

After our shift was over, Dunna and I sat up on the roof of one of the buildings in the compound, along with a few other members of the squad and about thirty of Jameed's mystery pills that I later learned were anti-psychotics. I took seven of them.

I hung out on the roof for a couple of hours joking with the guys. The other guys talked and I watched as their faces melted off and their heads morphed into reptilian monstrosities. Unable to handle the trip any longer, I went to my bunk and passed out. The dreams I had that night seemed to come right from one of gonzo artist Ralph Steadman's paintings.

The next day I was back in the tower with Jameed for the nightshift. He was obviously affected by the pills. For the first couple of hours, he sat quietly in the corner and looked scared shitless.

Eventually he worked up the courage to stand up and help keep a lookout. When he stood up, he noticed a small group of insurgents walking crouched in the grass toward our compound. He pointed them out to me and I looked through the thermal imaging scope to find them.

Not finding any hotspots, I explained to him that there weren't any insurgents in the field. He did not understand due to the language barrier and continued to flip out. I let him look through the scope but was still unable to appease him.

I turned around to call Kriesel on the radio and tell him I needed the 'terp to help me talk to Jameed. Kriesel radioed me back, saying that he would be up there in a minute with Timmy, the baby shrimp-sized 'terp. When I turned back around, Jameed was loading his RPK machine gun. I took his weapon away from him and set it down on the roof outside of the tower.

When Kriesel showed up with the 'terp, we tried to explain to Jameed that there were no enemies in the field. He insisted that there were, but we couldn't see them because every time we looked they would crouch down in the grass.

Sick of arguing with him, Kriesel tied a string to a chemlight and made Jameed wear it as a necklace. Then he told Jameed to go stand outside on the roof. Jameed understood that having a glowing thing attached to your body in the middle of the night on the roof of a building in an American military compound in Anbar Province was a sure way to get shot, so he went to bed instead. Having accomplished what he set out to do with the chemlight, Kriesel went back downstairs and talked to Jameed's supervisor.

When Kriesel was talking to Jameed's supervisor in the room where the Iraqis stayed, he found a pair of sunglasses that had been missing for a couple of days on Jameed's bed. Kriesel searched the room but didn't find anything else.

The next day, we started building a sandbag wall on the edge of the roof and around the towers. Kriesel put Jameed to work hauling sandbags up the stairs as punishment for stealing the glasses and for going apeshit the night before.

Jameed never sold us any more pills after that night, so we had to find other ways to keep from getting bored. Luckily, the neighbors provided some entertainment. One night we were using the forward-looking infrared (FLIR) camera to scan the area for activity. There was movement at the Flintstone's house, which was what we called the house across the canal from Pump House Barney, since Fred Flintstone is Barney Rubble's next-door neighbor. We zoomed in and saw that the family was all outside sleeping on the ground. When we zoomed in closer we realized that the parents were having sex. That is, at least one of them was trying to have sex; the wife wanted some dick but the guy seemed indifferent.

She started with a hand job. The detail in the FLIR was such that we could tell the guy was having some problems with erectile dysfunction. When the hand job failed to produce the desired result, she moved onto a blowjob. This produced results but the guy still seemed to not really give a shit.

"Goddamn, motherfucker needs to get on that shit," Sergeant Pinkney, a marine we had attached to our squad when we got to Iraq, commented. "If he doesn't get busy, pretty soon I'm going to have to swim across that canal and beat that shit up."

He finally got over his dysfunction, and his wife hiked up her burqa, jumped on him, and started riding him like a mechanical bull in a retro cowboy bar. She did that until she was satisfied and rolled off without the guy ever doing anything the entire time, except going flaccid every two or three minutes.

But other than Jameed's pills and Wilma Flintstone's randy midnight ride aboard Fred's semi-erect penis, our first stint at Pump House Barney was a two-week exercise in excruciating boredom.

CHAPTER 11:
Bye's IED

Q RF 2, THIS IS BRAVO X-RAY," our company ground operations center squawked over the radio.

"X-ray," I groaned into the microphone, pissed that I was going to have to get off the rock-hard mattress in my room in Fallujah and do something, "this is QRF 2. Send it."

"QRF 2 we need you to move to the QRF tent while QRF 1 is out."

"Roger, out," I responded, injecting my annoyance into my voice to make it clear that I wasn't pleased about having to get out of bed. I knew no one cared whether or not I was annoyed, but the futile gesture gave me a tiny bit of solace.

We'd been assigned to be part of a quick reaction force (QRF) in May 2006, about one month after we'd arrived in Iraq. Being on QRF 2 meant that we were the secondary quick reaction force, waiting to be called to duty while QRF 1 was making a run. Quick reaction forces were broken down into three twelve-hour shifts. QRF 1 was staged at the QRF tent, ready to move out the gate within minutes. Those on QRF 2 were normally in their rooms unless QRF 1 was out; then they were at the QRF tent, where quick reaction forces staged to roll out of the wire. QRF 3 was off unless some serious shit went down.

Working twelve-hour shifts made us irritable and angry. The first day or two of QRF seemed like some kind of sick joke, but after a couple of days, our moods became so foul that we could scrape resentment off our tongues. Being on QRF was like being in a prison, except that the bars had been replaced with radios. When we were on QRF, we carried radios everywhere we went in case we were called to go outside the wire. We carried the radio when we ate, while we slept, and even when we were jerking off in the porta-shitter. It was hard enough to concentrate on jerking off in those nasty plastic booths with the stench of shit and the rivers of sweat running down our faces distracting us; the cackling radio further dampened the mood. But we still got the job done. We were professionals, after all, members of the U.S. Armed Forces, the finest fighting and masturbating machines on the planet.

Most of us carried small handheld radios, but we took two-hour shifts carrying the advanced system improvement program (ASIP) radio, a large unit with a telephone-style receiver, and that afternoon I was in charge of carrying the big ASIP. After I got the call, I went to everyone's rooms, making them stop what they were doing and move over to the QRF tent. The rest of the squad was as pissed off as I was, and we drove our humvees to the QRF tent in complete silence.

We filtered inside the tent, doing our best to relax and break the grim mood that hung over us. I played cards with Grub, Horn, and Rystad. The other guys either laid down on the couches to watch a movie, or turned on their laptops to burn copies of the porn DVDs that had arrived in the latest care packages from home.

We had come to the QRF tent because QRF 1 had gone out to drop off a marine at Pump House Barney. The squad had left late in the afternoon. By the time it was driving back from Barney it was twilight—too dark to see the road well but too light to use night vision.

We hadn't been in the tent ten minutes when we got a call over the radio. "X-ray, this is QRF 1." It was Staff Sergeant Kerry Mandt, who was a squad leader in 3rd Platoon. "Our lead truck just hit an IED," he said.

The call ruined our attempts to relax and alleviate the tension that pressed down on everyone inside the tent. When we heard that the truck was disabled and there were injuries, we suited up and got in our humvees, knowing we were about to get a call to go out and help them. We were already on our way out the south gate before we got the call.

I drove one of our three humvees as fast as I could through Camp Fallujah, hitting speed bumps without slowing down. I hit one especially large speed

The humvee in which Sergeant Matthew Bye and Specialist Scott Stroud hit an IED, on base the day after the explosion.

bump hard, nearly ejecting Grub from the turret. He expressed his disapproval of my driving by kicking me in the head.

We'd already stopped at the south gate to load our weapons when we finally received the call: "QRF 2, this is X-ray. QRF 1 hit an IED on Route California." Route California was a shitty dirt road that paralleled the main service route (MSR) Mobile, a four-lane highway that ran from Fallujah to the south of Baghdad. Route California was lousy with IEDs, but our commanders, in their infinite wisdom, kept sending us down it. "You need to go assist them."

"Roger that X-ray," Nelly responded. "We're already at the south gate, over."

"Roger, X-ray out."

97

We hauled ass out of camp and were almost in sight of Mandt's squad when we got another call over the radio: "QRF 2, this is X-ray, you need to return to base to pick up an ambulance and a wrecker, over."

"Roger," Nelly said, annoyed that we had to leave Mandt's squad out there when we were so close. "We're on our way."

We got back to camp to find the ambulance waiting for us as X-ray had promised, but the wrecker was nowhere to be seen. "X-ray, this is QRF 2. There is no wrecker down here. Requesting permission to continue mission and get this ambulance out to the guys."

After a few minutes of deliberation, X-ray responded: "Roger. Go ahead and get that ambulance out there."

We rushed back to the site of the explosion with the ambulance following us. When we arrived, we stayed back and let the medics in the ambulance go to work. It was dark by then, and we couldn't see anything but camera flashes as Kriesel and Dunna took a few pictures of the blown-up humvee and the crater. Horn went over to find out what was happening and then came back to tell the rest of us: "Bye (Sergeant Matthew Bye, a team leader in Staff Sergeant Mandt's squad) got his legs all fucked up and Stroud (Specialist Scott Stroud, a crusty old guy who reenlisted to go to Bosnia after being out of the military for years) got some cuts and bruises."

The medics loaded Bye and Stroud into the ambulance. Later I learned that one of the medics had tried to give Bye an injection of morphine, but had been holding the injector upside down and accidentally injected himself with ten milligrams of it. Apparently this is a fairly common occurrence because all medics carry a morphine antidote, which he gave himself before he became totally wasted.

Kriesel and Nelly escorted the ambulance back to base with their humvees while Grub, Horn, and I stayed back to provide security for the destroyed humvee.

After a few minutes, the other two humvees returned to the explosion site with the explosive ordnance disposal (EOD) unit following close behind. An EOD is a unit that reacts to unexploded ordnance and IEDs. Its purpose is to destroy anything that hasn't already exploded and to analyze craters left by IEDs to find out what the enemy is using against us.

EOD figured out that the IED had been set off by a pressure device nicknamed "Christmas tree lights" because of their physical characteristics. We just called them "anal beads." When EOD finished its analysis of the site the unit drove back to base, and left us still waiting for a wrecker.

"X-ray, what is the status on that wrecker? Over," Nelly asked, frustrated that we were still sitting on the blast site.

"QRF 2, we are currently trying to find a wrecker that we can send out to you right now," X-ray squawked back. "As soon as we locate a wrecker we'll let you know. Until then just sit tight and keep that area secure." I wasn't surprised that they couldn't find a wrecker. I'd only been in Iraq about a month, but I'd already figured out that our commanders couldn't find their own rectums if they jammed GPS units up their asses.

We sat on the site for another four hours waiting for the commanders to figure out where to get a wrecker. When they finally found one to tow the wrecked humvee back to base, it was already 0100 and time for us to go out on QRF 1.

CHAPTER 12:
Blue on Blue

IN JUNE WE HEARD that our sister company, Alpha Company 2-136 Infantry, had a friendly fire incident. By then the cream of Alpha had been sent to Baghdad to serve out the rest of their deployment. The Alpha members who were left behind tended to be a bit on the special side—as in, "riding-the-short-bus" special. We weren't surprised to hear that they were involved in a friendly fire incident.

The military uses a color-code system for different forces, similar to the summer-camp color code system where boys are blue, girls are pink, and never should the two combine to make violet. The military marks coalition forces as blue and enemy forces as red, which, when mixed, make purple. Normally blue mixed with red, but apparently Alpha Company wanted to mix blue with blue to make a darker shade of blue.

The version of the story that I heard started with two Alpha Company Bradleys watching a road that ran through a junkyard one night. Their objective was to identify, engage, and destroy insurgents digging around for wire.

A marine patrol of three humvees drove through the junkyard after curfew. Like Alpha Company, the marines had been assigned to patrol the junkyard after dark and look for the same insurgents. Although they were on the same team, the guys in the Bradleys didn't know that the guys in the humvees would be there.

Mistaking the marine convoy of three very distinctive humvees for insurgents, the Alpha Company Bradleys attacked the marines. They began by firing the high-explosive ammunition in their 25mm machine guns at

Typical Iraqi vehicles look nothing like humvees, but that didn't stop Alpha Company from mistaking a marine humvee for a bongo truck.

the humvees. After Alpha Company had fired over fifty rounds, the marines were still alive and frantically moving around. Needing to get a kill out of the engagement, the Bradley commander ordered his gunner to fire the tube-launched optically-tracked wire-guided (TOW) missiles at them. The gunner fired one missile and missed, then fired a second missile, with similar results.

After launching the second missile, the Bradley commander called off the attack. The command center had called on the radio and explained that Alpha was firing at friendlies. Fortunately for the marines, the Alpha company gunners weren't very good shots—they'd fired fifty-three rounds of 25mm high-explosive ammo and two TOW missiles at the marines and missed completely. No marines were hurt and no humvees were damaged. Although we were all relieved that no one was injured in the engagement, it was a little disturbing to be fighting with a company that incompetent.

While Alpha was shooting at friendlies, we were earning the trust of local Iraqis.

Alpha fired rockets at U.S. marines. We rode bicycles.

The marines seemed to feel the same way, only they extended such sentiments to the entire Minnesota National Guard and not just Alpha. They began treating us worse than ever once word got out that a bunch of national guard shit-birds shot up a bunch of marines. We were already treated like a second-class force because we were national guard; after Alpha's mind-boggling screw up, they treated us like we were the most incompetent collection of fucktards in Anbar Province and they quit sending us out on any missions.

Our Bradleys sat parked in the back of our motor pool rusting, because we were not trusted to operate them lest we kill a bunch of marines. After about a month, a Marine Corps general walked by our motor pool and noticed the heavy vehicles in the back with tarps over them. He thought they could be useful in Habbaniyah, a shithole city halfway between Ramadi and Fallujah. So, our Bradleys patrolled the highways in and around Habbaniyah for about a month. During that month, we earned a reputation for being hardworking and competent. After that the marines treated us with respect.

About the same time our Bradleys began patrolling Habbaniyah, Colonel George H. Bristol became our new marine commander. A very large man standing about six feet three inches tall and weighing about two hundred and fifty pounds of solid muscle, Colonel Bristol made quite an impression on us. We saw him a lot more often than we'd ever seen Spineless Six Parks, a douchebag who knew we hated him and would only show up when absolutely necessary, make some pompous remarks, and then get the hell out of there as quickly as possible. Bristol made a point of circulating among his marines and (in our case) soldiers. He'd hang out in the motor pool or go out on patrol with us. Sometimes he'd just randomly show up, say some wild shit like, "I hunt men—God made me to hunt down evil men and kill them," then leave.

The more we got to know Bristol, the more we admired him. By the time he left us when his tour in Iraq was over, he had become an almost mythic figure to us.

When Bristol took over, he brought Sergeant Major Walter O'Connell with him. O'Connell was a tough old marine from Boston who was more concerned with the welfare of the soldiers in our company the first day he met us than any of our sergeant majors had ever been.

"Hey fellas," Sergeant Major O'Connell greeted us one day in his thick Boston accent in the chow hall. "How is that chow?"

"Hey sergeant major, the chow is good. How are you today?" Sergeant Everson replied. Like the rest of us, Eve's mouth was covered with a porn-star mustache. We were in the middle of a bad-mustache contest, and almost everyone at the table had a sleazy patch of pedophile hair growing on his upper lip.

"I'm doin' real well. I'm just getting up to get the boss some Diet Coke. You guys keep up all of the great work you're doing out there," he said before he walked away. "Oh, and by the way, shave those fucking mustaches. You look ridiculous."

When Bristol arrived in early August and heard about Bravo Company's work in Habbaniyah, he expanded our company's area of operation (AO) and sent us on daily foot and humvee patrols through the villages between camp and the Euphrates River.

Colonel George Bristol, a leader we so respected that any of us would have considered it an honor to have been killed by the man, rescued us from the purgatory we were stuck in after Alpha's blue-on-blue incident and sent us back on patrol outside the wire. *Eric Bowen*

106

Sergeant Major Walter O'Connell and Colonel Bristol came together as a package deal. *Eric Bowen*

Colonel Bristol quickly gained the respect of our company. Specialist Andrew Stockinger summed up our respect for the good colonel by saying: "I would feel privileged to be killed by this man." Bristol earned this respect by patrolling the same areas we did, staying at the pump house with us for a few days at a time, and just generally scaring the shit out of us instead of cowering behind a desk, like the Elicerio.

When Bristol was at Pump House Flanders with 3rd Squad, he walked into a room where Thorn and Ecker were playing a mutant version of war involving card stealing and physical abuse. When Bristol kicked the door off of its hinges (as a friend of Chuck Norris, this was Bristol's preferred method of entering a room), Ecker had Thorn at knifepoint, accusing him of cheating.

"Do you even know how to use that?" Bristol asked Ecker.

"I do on Thorn!" Ecker replied, ready to gut the scallywag for cheating.

"I've stabbed and I've been stabbed," Bristol said in his typical cryptic fashion. "I killed my first man at the age of twelve." Ecker and Thorn stared at Bristol, not knowing how to react, but comforted to know that the imposing figure standing in the doorway was on their side.

CHAPTER 13:
Neumiller Cooking Meth

M AURSTAD, I CAN'T BELIEVE THIS!" Neumiller said, walking out of the door of the post exchange (PX) just as I was about to walk in.

"What's going on, Neumiller?"

"They just sold me a shitload of Sudafed," Neumiller replied. "I would be in jail if I tried to buy all of this back home!" I knew this was the beginning of something really bad, because Sudafed is a decongestant that contains ephedrine, which is one of the key ingredients in making meth.

Sure enough, once Neumiller got his hands on all that Sudafed, he started cooking methamphetamine in his barracks room. This was in early August and Neumiller was sick of drinking Robitussin cough syrup to get his fix.

If Neumiller had used the same degree of resourcefulness he put into his illegal activities to make something of his life, he would likely have became a successful businessman. But the only things that seemed to spur him into action always involved committing at least one felony. To accomplish his latest hobby—the manufacture of meth in the tight confines of his barracks under the watchful eyes of Sergeant First Class Rogers, our platoon sergeant—required every bit of resourcefulness that Neumiller had at his disposal. Fortunately for Neumiller, Rogers' attitude was "you leave me alone and I'll leave you alone." As long as we didn't bother him while he was in his room playing *Warcraft III* on his computer, Neumiller was free to engage in whatever felonious enterprise intrigued him at the moment.

We took this photo around Independence Day, 2006. Neumiller was not in the picture, most likely because he was busy cooking meth.

To start his barracks meth lab, he pilfered Windex from the cleaning supplies closet and WD-40 from the mechanics in the motor pool. He used an intricate system of baby food jars mailed from the States, a water heater, and empty Powerade bottles to build the apparatus for cooking the meth. He kept this amateur chemistry set under his bed to hide it from anyone who might give a shit.

He spent months researching how to cook meth without certain chemicals not easily accessible in a third-world, war-torn country. He searched the internet, called old friends from his drug-addled civilian days, and conducted his own chemistry experiments. When he finally figured out a workable combination of chemicals, he started stocking up on Sudafed, sending accomplices to the PX to keep suspicion down.

When the cooking operation was underway, Neumiller had a little more trouble keeping his criminal venture quiet. A common problem with meth cooking is that some of the chemicals react badly if not properly cooked together, causing explosions. Soldiers in the middle of fighting a war aren't prone to ratting one another out, but it's hard to have a quiet explosion inside a barracks.

The first time Neumiller's meth lab exploded, he ran out of his room holding a Powerade bottle filled with rancid liquid that was expanding rapidly. He ran into the bathroom and dropped the bottle into the toilet, then jumped out of the bathroom just in time to avoid the chemical explosion.

The meth explosion filled the barracks with a bleach-like stench for the rest of the day. For some reason, no one questioned what was going on. If anyone else did know what he was doing, no one really seemed to care.

Several explosions and assorted misadventures later, Neumiller got his hands on a bottle of absinthe. That night he and Yogi drank the bottle in one sitting. The absinthe hit Neumiller hard and he went a little crazy, deciding that he needed to kill Horn. He loaded a magazine into his rifle, chambered a round, and left the room to go shoot Horn. Yogi cut Neumiller off in the hall and knocked him out to keep him from committing murder, even though Yogi wasn't very fond of Horn either.

When Neumiller regained consciousness, he found a shower curtain rod and tried to hit Yogi with it. All of the commotion woke Sergeant Marshall Tanner, a Bradley commander in our platoon. Tanner walked outside of the barracks to see Neumiller crying and swinging the curtain rod at Yogi, who was trying his best not to use his giant Uzbek arms to crush the sniveling little brat.

Eventually Yogi got sick of dealing with Neumiller and swung at him with full force. The punch missed, leaving the lucky little meth addict's head still attached to his body. When Yogi's punch went wide, Tanner grabbed Neumiller from behind, body slammed him into the pavement, and subdued him until First Sergeant Eggert was summoned. No one realized what a mistake it would be to enlist Top's help in dealing with Neumiller.

Top took the whining bitch into a room and questioned him about what went on that night. Top gave him a pen and a notebook, and told him to name

Neumiller was in trouble early and often. He is seen here doing flutter kicks with his rifle suspended above him for fucking up in Camp Shelby.

names of individuals who were using steroids or pot. Neumiller, in true meth addict form, narc'ed out just about every person in our unit, whether he knew they were doing something illegal or not. Some were guilty as hell, but many, if not most, had done nothing wrong. This is a list of some of the people and charges, in no particular order:

- Sergeant Jay Horn, steroids
- Staff Sergeant Tim Nelson, steroids
- Specialist Gib Trontvet, steroids
- Specialist Oleg Yagudayev, steroids
- Specialist Bryan McDonough, steroids
- Sergeant John Kriesel, steroids/pot
- Specialist Isaac Pratt, pot
- Specialist Jason Klimek, pot
- Specialist Ben Doran, pot
- Specialist Jermaine Kowalenko, steroids

Oleg "Yogi" Yagudayev serving up a cold bowl of fuck.

The accused were stripped of their weapons, as was Neumiller, and none of them were allowed to work. Meanwhile, the rest of the company worked extra hours to make up for their absences. We had eleven guys out of the work rotation and several more who were on leave, so everyone remaining had to work even harder, longer, and more often.

As the investigation progressed, it became clear that most of the people on Neumiller's bullshit blacklist were innocent. Most of the guys were given back their rifles and sent to work. Soon Top started to look like the fanatical loon that he was. This became especially clear when one of his superiors questioned him about what he was doing and he replied, "I take pride in taking down my own guys!"

Kriesel spends some quality time with his deployment wife.

He went into Gib's room and confiscated all of the protein supplements that Gib was taking to help him with his weight lifting. This was why Neumiller had accused him of taking steroids.

"You don't need any of this stuff to get big," Top lectured Gib. "You just need to work out hard and eat a lot of steak, and in a year or two you will have a body like this." Top puffed up his chest, which wasn't nearly as impressive as he seemed to think it was.

Repulsed by Top, who was flexing his saggy old pectorals to show how Gib could look one day if he had enough drive and determination, Gib protested, "I bought those at the PX. They aren't steroids."

"Well, we will just see about that when the results of your piss test come back."

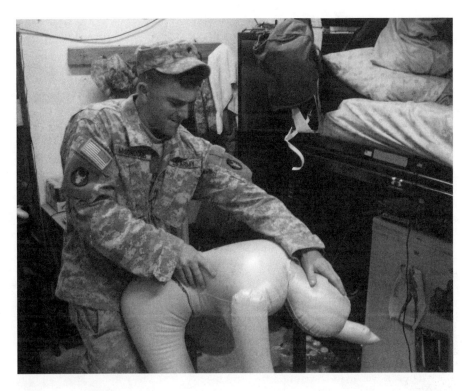

What Kriesel didn't know was that his deployment wife was having a steamy affair with McDonough.

The official story was that the urine test samples were mistakenly destroyed on the plane headed for the States, where they would be analyzed. It is generally accepted, though, that Sergeant Major O'Connell, sick of Top's bullshit, stomped the box before it was shipped. If anyone was actually using steroids, no one was busted for it.

Yogi, Neumiller, and Token were all busted down in rank for being drunk the night Neumiller flipped out. Yogi received the worst of the punishments—not only because he was drunk, but also because he assaulted Neumiller. (In retrospect, it seemed Yogi would have been better off not to step in that night, but to just let Neumiller murder Horn.)

The investigation even turned up other charges that weren't part of Neumiller's accusations. Pratt, a fister in 2nd Platoon, was busted for having a pistol that he bought from an Iraqi and carried as a side arm. The unauthorized weapon got him into a significant amount of trouble and cost him rank and pay.

Neumiller lost some rank and pay, but because of his willingness to cooperate (in other words, lie and accuse other people of breaking the rules), he got a lighter punishment. His weapon was returned before most of the other guys were put back to work. Captain Murphy wanted to send Neumiller back to our squad, but Nelly convinced him that if Neumiller came back to our squad, Yogi would kill him the first time they went outside the wire and his body would be disposed of in the Euphrates River, never to be seen again. Murphy relented and sent Neumiller to work for the mechanics.

Wallace approached me after the Neumiller meltdown and told me about a betting pool that had been started in Camp Shelby. Wallace and some of the other guys had made bets on who would be the first person to snap once we got into Iraq.

"You really surprised me, Maurstad," Wallace said. "I thought for sure you would be the one to snap. I lost ten bucks because of you."

"Why the hell did you think I would be the first one to lose it?" I asked.

"Because you are always walking around by yourself and you look so fucking pathetic all of the time. I mean, I love ya, bro, but you have looked like you were close to snapping since we were in Shelby."

"I'm sorry to disappoint you." We had a good laugh about what a crazy dipshit Neumiller was and I went to chow.

Wallace had a point about me being somewhat of a loner. For the past six weeks I had been eating chow by myself. It was a ritual I started in order to get away from the people who surrounded me literally 24/7. I walked to the chow hall by myself and ate without talking to anyone. When I was finished eating I stayed at my table for thirty to sixty minutes watching the news. If I met one of the other guys walking out of the chow hall, it would be okay to walk and talk with them on my way back to the barracks, but I considered my brief time alone everyday somewhat sacred.

I continued my ritual that day like any other day. I was walking quietly to chow when Top met me.

"Hey Merstad," Top said, mispronouncing my name even though he had known me for almost four years.

A boat ferries people across the Euphrates.

"Hi Top," I replied quietly as I walked past him, trying my best to stick to my routine.

"Hey! Get back here!"

"Yes, first sergeant?"

"Do you have some kind of a fucking problem with me?"

"No, first sergeant." The truth was that I did have a problem with the fact that Top had incapacitated our entire platoon because some junkie had ratted out a bunch of innocent people, but I wasn't about to tell him that.

"Where do you get off treating me with such disrespect?"

"I didn't realize that I had, first sergeant."

"You're telling me that when you walk by without even greeting me or any senior NCO, you aren't being disrespectful?"

"I did, first sergeant."

"Now you are lying to me? What the fuck is your problem, Merstad? Do you just have a case of the I-don't-want-to-fucking-be-here-todays, or should

I start targeting you too?" Even though his investigation had fallen apart, it didn't seem like Top was ready to give up his witch hunt just yet.

"I'm fine, first sergeant," I said, trying to get the prick off of my case. "I'm sorry."

"Well I am going to have a talk with your squad leader when I get back and we will figure out what to do with you," Top said, calming down a little bit. "Get out of here."

I continued with my routine, though now I was pissed off. When I finished chow I walked back to the barracks to play *Ghost Recon Advanced Warfighter* on my Xbox 360. I met Top again as he was leaving my barracks building, presumably after having a talk about me with my squad leader.

"Get your hands out of your pockets," he scolded me.

"Good evening, first sergeant," I responded taking my hands out of my pockets.

The verbal abuse that followed lasted for over five minutes. During the ass-chewing he tried to make himself feel tough by pushing me a couple of times with his fat gut and yelling less than an inch from my face. The close proximity caused the tobacco-filled spit flying from his mouth to hit me in the face.

"*Do you understand me!*" yelled the first sergeant, concluding his verbal tirade.

"Yes, first sergeant, perfectly clear," I replied, having blocked out everything that he had just been yelling. I went into the barracks to find everyone standing in the hall, wondering what the hell was going on.

"Top was pissed about something, I don't really know what." I really didn't know what he was saying. I'd willed my brain to shut off the entire time the lunatic ranted and raved at me. I went to my happy place, which was back home, lying in the grass in my old man's front yard. "I wasn't paying attention."

CHAPTER 14:
Whips, Chains, and Hot Wax

I<small>N LATE</small> A<small>UGUST</small> 2006 I <small>WENT HOME</small> on leave and didn't return until mid-September. Not much happened while I was gone. The intense late-summer heat probably took the piss out of the insurgents just as it took it out of us. The most exciting thing that happened was that EOD blew up a dead cow on the side of the road. Horn and the rest of my squad found the cow's carcass on the road by a village called Al Mehr. They figured it was nothing too dangerous and it most likely didn't hide an IED, but they called in EOD

A bloated cow on the road. This could conceivably conceal an IED, so the only sensible thing to do was blow it up.

The robot used to drop the C-4 charge.

The cow blows up real good.

anyway just because they wanted to watch EOD blow it up. That was EOD's solution to pretty much everything: blow it up with some C-4. The bigger and squishier the thing they were blowing up, the more fun it was to watch, and things don't get much bigger or squishier than a dead cow bloated in the hot August Iraqi sun.

The day I got back I went straight to Pump House Flanders. As soon as Horn saw me, he said, "Maurstad, I'm glad you're back. Go burn the shit."

"Fuck you. I just got back from leave."

"I don't care," he said. "You're still going to go burn shit."

"But it's not my shit," I said.

"Just go burn it." So I went to burn shit.

We had porta-shitters at the pump houses, but instead of the normal tanks, these had barrels underneath the seats. We'd shit until the barrels were full, then we'd haul the barrels out, dump them into a pit, and light them on fire. We'd soak the whole mess in JP8, jet fuel that was sort of like diesel but didn't light very easily. To get it to burn, we'd put some paper on top of the stinking mess and light it on fire with matches. It reminded me of when we got bored back on the farm and burned useless shit. But real shit—actual feces—smelled a hell of a lot worse.

Mmmmm. Smells like Jameed.

Once we got it burning, we'd stir it up to make sure that it burned completely. It was a horrible, stinking job, but normally I didn't mind doing it because I'd contributed my own feces to the mess. This time it was especially disgusting because none of the shit was my own—I hadn't been back long enough to dump out yet.

After I burned the shit, I went on tower shift. Later that evening we got intel that a possible attack might take place the next morning. Apparently there was a truck with an antiaircraft gun and it was going to attack us. *Ah, fuck:* I thought. *My first day back from leave and I have to burn someone else's shit, then I get to die.*

I went back on tower shift at midnight. There was no moon and I couldn't see a damned thing. I'd lost my complacency after being home for three weeks and I was nervous. To make matters worse, they put me in the scary tower. We called it "the scary tower" because it was on a part of the pump house that was built into a hill, so it sat just about at ground level facing the canal. To the right was a road that gave insurgents easy access to the tower. We felt like sitting ducks in the scary tower.

I sat white-knuckled in the scary tower, waiting for the insurgents to come and kill me with their truck-mounted antiaircraft gun, and listening to coyotes dig around in the garbage outside the wire. Suddenly, marine Corporal Chris Ness popped up at the door. Not knowing who it was, I pointed my rifle at him. "Whoa! Whoa! It's cool!" he said.

"Jesus Christ, man. You can't sneak up on me like that. It's my first day back from leave."

"Oh. Well, I just came back to tell you we're going to shoot off some flares."

"Thanks," I said, "but if you come back here again, let me know you're coming because I just about shot you in the face."

"All right. No problem. See you later."

After my tower shift ended, I spent a couple of hours sitting in another tower with Corey, watching for the insurgents in the attack truck. We were both pretty nervous about the imminent attack.

"It's fucked up that we only have a .50-caliber machine gun," I said, "and they have an antiaircraft gun that's more powerful than any weapons we have in this tower." We had a couple of AT4 antitank missiles in another tower, but because our tower was the most likely to be attacked first, we didn't get any of the good weapons. "If they fire one shot at us and we survive, fucking run."

"I'm cool with that," Corey said. We sat for the next couple of hours waiting for the attack that never came.

After that we were put on QRF. About a week later a Bradley hit an IED on the southern edge of our AO. Our AO had been expanded while I was gone, and we went to an area where I'd never been before. We escorted an M88 recovery vehicle, a heavily-armored tracked vehicle with a huge winch and

A Bradley sunk into a ditch, missing its left track.

boom that's used to recover everything up to and including the M1 Abrams tank. Basically it's an oversized, heavily armored tow truck on tracks. We also brought a flatbed truck to haul the destroyed Bradley back to camp.

I went out in a humvee with Grub, Horn, and Specialist Hans von Schlichtling (not exactly his real name—if I used his real name, his wife would kill him in his sleep). I was driving, Grub was manning the gun, Horn was sitting beside me in the passenger seat, and von Schlichtling was in the back. Von Schlichtling was a little older than the rest of us, in his late twenties or early thirties. His upper body was scrawny, almost atrophied, but he had a huge pot belly. Then he went back to being scrawny from the ass down. He looked sort of like an avocado pit with tooth picks stuck in it. He looked like a fucking chomo (child molester), but really he was an all-right guy. Nelly gave him the nickname "Bat Wing," but after he started liking that name too much—he took to carrying around a rubber bat—we changed his nickname to "von Schlichtlingstein" (not exactly his real nickname, but close) which had to be pronounced with a heavy German accent, complete with lots of guttural noises and spitting.

When we got to the Bradley we sat in the humvee and waited for the mechanics to lift it up with the M88. While we waited, Horn started

A humvee providing security.

fucking with von Schlichtlingstein. Von Schlichtlingstein's wife could charitably be described as Rubenesque. Horn asked von Schlichtlingstein if he had a picture of his wife.

"Yeah, here," von Schlichtlingstein said. "What do you think? Pretty nice?"

"Yeah, she's good looking," Horn said. "I like a woman with a little extra meat on her bones." Horn's wife weighed maybe 105 pounds after a huge meal, so we knew he was full of shit.

"I don't really like those skinny women," von Schlichtlingstein said. "They gross me out."

"I hear you, man," Horn said. "I bet you can't wait to get back home and fuck her again."

"Yeah, I can't wait. It's going to be great."

"What kind of stuff are you into?" Horn asked.

"Some pretty wild shit. We really enjoy some play with whips and hot wax." Von Schlichtlingstein was dead serious. By this time Grub and I were in tears laughing, but von Schlichtlingstein couldn't see us. Horn was barely keeping it together.

"I hear you, man," Horn said. "That's some good stuff. I like the whips and chains myself. Do you ever do anything else?"

"We haven't done it yet," von Schlichtlingstein said, "but we'd be really interested in a swap sometime."

"That's cool," Horn said, then changed the subject before von Schlichtlingstein could suggest he and Horn swapped wives. We'd do just about anything to keep each other amused amid the excruciating boredom, but climbing on top of Mrs. von Schlichtlingstein for our amusement was a greater sacrifice than Horn was willing to make.

CHAPTER 15:
Pump House Barney

A FTER A COUPLE OF WEEKS ON QRF, I was temporarily reassigned. Two guys from 1st Squad were doing some training, so Lance Corporal Bruce Miller and I got attached to their squad for a couple of days to fill in for them. We went to Pump House Barney in the middle of the afternoon and replaced the squad from 3rd Platoon.

"It has been really nice out here," Sergeant Johnson, one of the team leaders from 3rd Platoon, told Sergeant Goldstein on the way out of the compound. We called Johnson "the sawed-off sergeant" because he looked to be a tick over five feet tall, but he was a great guy and a good NCO. "We haven't been attacked in twenty-one days." Goldstein didn't like hearing this. It was his first day back from leave and the outpost was overdue for an attack. He figured it would be his typical shitty luck to get shot the day he got back to Iraq.

When we got to Barney I went to one of the towers to work the first four-hour shift, while newly promoted Sergeant Jake Brown worked in the other tower. When I got into my tower I took my helmet off, set up a comfortable place to sit, and began reading a copy of *Maxim*. I forgot to bring my personal radio, which meant I couldn't make the shift go faster by engaging Brown in pointless banter.

I spent the first few minutes of my tower shift enjoying the sunny, 90-degree Iraqi autumn evening, but before I could get too relaxed, three shots from what sounded like a semi-automatic grenade launcher interrupted my peace. The shots sounded like they'd come from Brown's tower. Brown was

First Squad trying to beat the heat at Barney.

My tower at Barney contained three ready-to-fire machine guns.

always trying to find imaginative ways to occupy his time, so some grenade launcher practice didn't seem out of the question.

I looked out of the window and watched the rounds explode in the field to our south on the other side of the canal. Explosions—at least friendly explosions—always provide an awesome spectacle.

After the explosions I looked out at Brown's tower to see if he would launch any more, but saw the door on Brown's tower closed and the grenade launcher leaning against the sandbag wall. Annoyed that we were under attack, I put my helmet back on just in time to see two rocket-propelled grenade (RPG) vapor trails appear between our towers. The two grenades

Lance Corporal Bruce Miller is all kinds of happy after firing the SAW during the attack on Pump House Barney.

exploded in the field behind us, where the mortars had landed a couple of minutes earlier.

Realizing that this was going to be a serious attack and not just the few badly aimed mortars that we'd grown accustomed to, I looked for the source of the attack. I stuck my head out of the window with a pair of binoculars and scanned the area for something threatening to shoot.

Once my head was exposed, the enemy opened fire with AK-47s. I pulled my head back into the tower when I heard the rounds snapping around me and hitting my tower. I got behind a sheet of bulletproof glass and scanned

131

Rystad and Grub drink some water after the march to cool off.

the area, but couldn't see where the shooting was coming from. Brown started shooting a M240B from his tower, but I still couldn't find the enemy.

"Where the fuck are they shooting from!" I yelled down to Sergeant Cannon Yang. Yang put his arms up signaling that he didn't know. "Send someone up here with me," I yelled. "I don't have a radio."

Cannon didn't hear the last thing I yelled at him and I was alone in my tower until the end of the five-minute firefight. Then Goldstein and navy Corpsman John Bringel came into my tower; Bringel checked me out to make sure I was okay while Goldstein scanned the area looking for a second attack.

When the shooting finally stopped I couldn't stop shaking from the adrenaline. Brown, having done all of the shooting in the engagement, was physically sick and puking from the adrenaline, so Bringel left my tower to take care of him. Goldstein stayed in my tower and talked about his shitty luck of being shot at the day he got back to Iraq and how Johnson had jinxed us. After Goldstein left I finished my tower shift, pissed that I couldn't read my magazine or take my helmet off.

The next day our squad showed up with the two guys from 1st Squad to relieve Miller and me. We stayed at Barney, using it as a patrol base to walk through nearby villages. Miller and I were given the rest of the day off since we had both done a tower shift.

We joined our squad the next morning on what would come to be known as Horn's death march. We set off on our walk at 1000 and walked about a mile to the nearest bridge to cross the canal, searching for weapons caches on the banks of the canal the entire way.

We crossed the bridge and took a break by searching a couple of houses and talking to some locals. I sat in the shade, providing security while most of the others went inside the house. The Iraqis who drove by looked at us with contempt. We were the first military patrol to go south of that canal in nearly six months.

After the twenty-minute break, we walked through fields looking for weapons and mortar pits on our way to the next village. Horn led the march with Grub, Miller, and me not far behind. Horn kept a grueling pace while leading us through mud and soft, freshly tilled dirt. It was one hundred degrees and we were miserable, lugging our heavy gear with six inches of mud caked to the bottom of our boots. A little ways further into the muddy fields, we had to start jumping canals. With my track record jumping in full gear, I was secretly glad to see Grub and Horn fall into canals before I did. Having wet boots and pants made them even more miserable, while the squad's water consumption lightened my pack.

For the first time during the deployment I managed to jump every obstacle without falling. We marched through another village filled with people who looked upset by our presence.

When we got through the second village, we crossed a canal that was too large to jump by carefully walking across a narrow valve. This was nearly impossible to accomplish in full gear, so we threw our packs across and passed our rifles to the other side to free our hands.

We made it across without a problem until Specialist Hoiland, who'd joined our platoon as a Bradley gunner after some of our original gunners had been sent home with injuries, slipped off the valve and soaked one of his legs. He tried to catch himself on the handle that raised and lowered the gate, but couldn't.

Ferris, who had joined our squad after the steroid fiasco, crossed last. Ferris managed to fuck up just about anything he attempted—he lost his rifle once, his night-vision goggles twice, and pretty much sucked at everything he did. But what happened next wasn't really his fault. He did everything the same as those before him had done. He grabbed the handle and used it to hold himself up as he maneuvered around it. The handle, weakened by Hoiland's fall, bent and Ferris fell backwards into the canal, soaking his uniform and all his gear.

Once everyone was across the canal, we walked into a palm grove to rest for a few minutes. We were about four miles into our walk and still had another village to hit before we would start walking back.

"What kind of a fucked up place has palm trees with no paradise?" Horn asked as the squad relaxed in the shade of the palm trees.

It didn't take long for Nelly to realize that the squad was too tired to walk another mile, let alone all the way back, so he called the Bradleys to come and get us. We packed into the back of the Brads when they arrived, happy to be getting a ride.

When we got back to Barney we took off our gear and stood in the breeze with our sweaty clothes to cool off. All of us looked like we had just jumped into a swimming pool with our clothes on.

We changed into fresh clothes, cleaned up, and spent the rest of the day lying in our beds resting for the next morning, when we'd have to go out and do it all over again.

"Hey Rystad," Horn said, "I bet if you put a diaper on your aunt she'd look like a baby." Horn was referring to Corey's aunt, who was a little person, although everyone in our squad except Corey used the less-sensitive term "midget." I had personally stopped teasing him about it when I saw how upset it made him.

Sergeant Jay Horn, our team leader, demonstrates his celebrated oral pleasure technique on a piece of watermelon.

He told Horn to fuck himself, which prompted Mad Max, a seventeen-year-old Iraqi from Baghdad who'd learned English in high school and worked with us as a 'terp, to join in. He started making jokes that didn't really make sense due to his vague grasp of the English language. It was still highly effective in agitating Corey, as the word midget sounded hilarious with Max's accent: "Meejer."

Once Nelly figured that Corey had taken enough abuse for one day, he put an end to it and we started asking Max what he was going to do when he got to the States. "Man, I'm going to get drunk and fuck all of that nice,

Max leans against a tower thinking about all of the loose American pussy he hopes to get one day.

loose American pussy." We tried to explain to him that loose pussy was bad and he would really prefer some tight pussy. Being just a kid and not yet understanding much about sex or the female anatomy, he insisted that he really wanted some loose American pussy. After several failed attempts, we quit trying to convince him otherwise.

CHAPTER 16:
Raven

HEY MAURSTAD," NELLY SAID ONE DAY about a week after I finished working with 1st Squad, "you're going to stay back from the pump house for a couple of days so you can learn to fly the Raven." We used the Raven miniature unmanned aerial vehicle (MUAV) as a separate patrol. Our normal Raven pilot, Sergeant Dan Nygard, flew it around areas we weren't patrolling, looking for unusual activity. Nygard was our only Raven pilot, but because he worked an eight-hour shift in the operations center every day, he had very limited time to fly it. To get more flight time from the Raven, Captain Rankin had Nygard and some guy from Camp TQ come and teach six of the dismounts (infantry soldiers who weren't assigned to Bradley crews) how to operate it. Nelly informed me that I was one of the six.

The Raven is an electric, remote-controlled airplane that can fly up to six miles away from the operator at a speed of thirty to sixty miles per hour and up to an altitude of one thousand feet. It has a wingspan of just over 4 feet, a length of 3 1/2 feet, and weighs about 4 pounds. The U.S. military purchased five thousand of them at a cost of $35,000 each. And I destroyed two of them.

Our training consisted of one day of classroom instruction in the use of the Raven's computer navigation system, and two days of flight instruction in an open area of camp. We practiced launching and landing, circling a target, and calculating the position of a target from the altitude and the GPS location of the aircraft. Once we learned the essentials of flying the Raven effectively,

Me holding the Raven, doing preflight checks on the roof of a building at Flanders.

One of the Ravens that I broke planted firmly in the ground after a nosedive landing.

This wall should consider itself lucky just to get pissed on; Grub relieved his bowels on the roof of every Iraqi house we ever stayed in.

we were allowed to take it out and fly missions. I was the only one who ever flew with any regularity besides Nygard.

I didn't get a chance to use the Raven for a couple of months after our initial training. Nygard had been taking all of the flying missions and I was too busy working at observation posts (OPs) to spend any precious time off flying. I finally got the chance to fly it when Lieutenant Blomgren asked if it could be used to provide aerial reconnaissance for the OPs. This seemed like a perfect opportunity to get out of going to the OP and still help my squad, so I told him that the Raven would be ideal for that sort of work. Of course I volunteered to do the flying. He wanted me to drag all the gear to the OP, but I explained that it would be difficult to drag all the gear there and that I could be just as productive flying it from Flanders.

Kriesel watches news coverage of Saddam Hussien's sentencing in an Iraqi house while the 'terp translates.

The next time my squad went on a night OP, I stayed back at Flanders and flew the Raven—or at least I intended to fly the Raven. Yogi stayed back with me to be my co-pilot. We lugged all of the gear onto the roof of the barracks and set up the equipment.

Yogi assembled the seven-piece plane while I put the antenna up and started the computer. Once everything was put together, we did the pre-flight checks. The plane was in good shape and ready to go, but the computer couldn't establish a GPS link.

I restarted the computer and disassembled and reassembled everything in an attempt to repair it. Finally I gave up. I couldn't fly the plane without GPS. Yogi and I decided to go to bed and try again in the morning.

I woke up at the crack of noon and started the whole process over again, arriving at the exact same result. We talked it over and decided that it wasn't worth trying any longer, so I read a book while Yogi worked out in our makeshift gym.

The rest of the squad came back to Flanders just after dark. I tried to bullshit Nelly when he asked if I had flown at all, but I was busted when he asked where I had been flying.

A couple of days later I was asked to fly around the school at CP checkpoint 36, which was an intersection near El Namer where there was a small shop, a school, and a mosque filled with people who didn't like us very much. The rest of the squad would be inside the school talking to people. I was supposed to make sure no one snuck up on them.

Again Yogi stayed at Flanders with me while the rest of the squad went to the school on foot. We set everything up and got the pre-flight checks done without any trouble. I gave Yogi a quick lesson on how to launch the plane and demonstrated throwing it.

It took off without any problems and we ran our first flight down to the school to see if anyone was around. We checked the nearby mosque and small store before coming back to change the battery. The first landing went well and it appeared that I was going to have a good day flying.

Yogi got the battery changed out while I set up the computer for a longer flight. When everything was ready, Yogi said that he wanted to try launching it. I reluctantly agreed, figuring he would do fine being a strong and athletic person.

He stood on the edge of the flat roof and held the plane just as I had. He took a few quick steps and threw the plane. It struggled to pick up enough speed to lift itself into the air and eventually nosedived into the reeds above a swamp. To make matters worse, the swamp was created from the drain on the urinal.

Yogi stopped giggling when I told him that there was no way in hell I would go down to dig the plane out of the piss swamp. He walked out toward the plane on a culvert, doing a balancing act trying not to fall. I watched as he managed to retrieve the plane without touching any piss and keeping the plane itself piss free.

Glad to have the plane still in working order, I let Yogi redeem himself with a second attempt. He got it into the air without any trouble, and I flew around a nearby village until the battery needed changing again.

I brought the plane in for my second landing the same way I did it the first time. I dropped altitude by flying in a wide circle and bringing it in just above a tall set of highline wires. Things went well until the plane lost link with my controller, seemingly for no reason whatsoever. It was three-quarters through the last circle and decided to land all by itself. I watched through the viewfinder as the plane glided itself into the only water puddle for twenty-five miles in any direction.

Yogi and I walked out to find the non-waterproof aircraft completely submersed. The electronics were fried, ruining the plane. (One plane down, one to go . . .)

We walked back and set the plane in the sun with the access panel open, hoping that the electronics would dry out and somehow start working again. (They didn't.) Yogi had already assembled the other plane to curb the boredom of watching me fly.

Without wasting any more time, we put the second bird into the air. Yogi's throw was poor once again, but the plane managed to recover just a few inches before crashing into the piss swamp. I flew to the school to check on the guys before flying down some roads to see what traffic was out that day.

The first road I flew down was Route Panama. I looked at a shop alongside the road and checked out a couple of IED hotspots. When I had flown for about two miles, I turned around and flew back on a parallel road across the canal. I flew about two hundred meters before I saw a blue bongo truck (a little open-bed delivery-type truck that was popular in Iraq) sitting in an intersection with four guys digging in the road in front of the truck. I told Yogi to get on the computer and start capturing images of the guys while I tried to figure out exactly where I was. Yogi went down to the radio shack to report the insurgents and to call in artillery fire to kill them. I was on the roof, still struggling to figure out exactly where the plane was.

Yogi yelled up that we had clearance for an artillery strike if I could get a definite position on the enemy. Just as I figured out what intersection I was looking at, three of the men ran in one direction while the truck drove down the road right to checkpoint 36, where Nelly was.

Sometimes the insurgents would blow themselves up with the IED they just planted. We appreciated their cooperation.

Yogi called Nelly and told him to stop the truck that was coming toward him on South Canal Road, while I kept following the truck with the Raven.

I watched from above as the rest of the squad pulled the uncooperative enemy from his truck and roughed him up a little bit before putting some zip cuffs on him. A search of the truck revealed what could be called an IED starter kit—everything a young insurgent needs to blow up Americans.

High on my fresh accomplishment, I flew the plane back to Flanders while most of the squad walked back to pick up the humvees. A couple of people were left to guard the bongo truck so we could take it back to base and have the military police (MP) search it as a crime scene.

I was bringing the plane in for a landing just as the guys were coming into the pump house. After I completed my altitude drop, I tried to fly the plane

Staff Sergeant Tim "Nelly" Nelson finds an IED starter kit in the back of the bongo truck.

over the highline wires. I had a hard time judging the relationship between the plane and the tower that held the wires up, and the plane crashed and fell to the ground about a kilometer away from the pump house. Two planes flown, two destroyed—a perfect record!

Nelly and Horn came onto the roof to tell me what a good job I had done and to find out how long it would take me to get everything packed up to leave. Immediately afterwards, they hurled a tirade of insults and curses at me when I explained that I'd fucked up the landing and it would be at least fifteen minutes before I could leave.

I was told to get a ride back with Jones, whose squad was doing a foot patrol out of the pump house in the opposite direction of ours. Nelly and Horn left with the rest of the squad to go pick up the bongo truck and return to base.

Horn sits with the defeated insurgent. The young Iraqi looks like he is in tough shape, but he is lucky to be alive.

Yogi and I walked back out into the field, retrieved the damaged plane, and went back to Flanders to pack everything up. Just as we finished, Jones arrived and told me to get my ass in gear and pack my shit into the humvee.

When we got back to our compound on Camp Fallujah Captain Rankin met Yogi and me and commended us on a job well done. He was pleased with the so-far unproductive Raven's capture of an enemy. He didn't even mind that I had destroyed all of the company's Ravens in the process. He reassured me, "That's just the cost of doing business."

CHAPTER 17:

Thanksgiving 2006

IN NOVEMBER 2006, A CREW OF SEABEES (the construction engineers of the navy) came to Flanders to build a third barracks building. We needed it to house a second squad that would use the small outpost as a base for conducting foot patrol of nearby villages.

While the Seabees were there, they installed a chain link fence on top of the ten-foot concrete walls that surrounded the compound. This was to catch RPGs that came over the walls, which had recently become a problem. Third squad had an RPG bounce off of pipes and walls like a pinball machine before sailing right past three people's heads and blowing up a pallet of MREs.

This would earn both Fish and Hassel Purple Hearts, although Fish was the only one who legitimately deserved one. He had taken shrapnel in his arm, while Hassel had gotten a concussion and most people agree that he had exaggerated his wounds. We gave him a hard time for receiving a Purple Heart for his little bump on the head, good naturedly at first, but with more resentment after other people started to get seriously wounded and killed.

The Seabees worked hard from sun up to sun down every day that they were out there. This was in marked contrast to the Marine Corps engineers, who seemed to show up, do a couple hours of work, eat all of our food, and leave. On one occasion the marines showed such disregard for our food supply that they left us in a serious bind. They ate so much that we were almost completely out of food four days before we were scheduled to leave Pump House Barney and we had to call for an early re-supply.

Despite having our food supply pillaged by marines on a regular basis, we kept morale up. Kriesel contributed to group morale in his usual creepy fashion, which involved him parading around in the nude. Kriesel introduced us to Big Jim and the twins after we'd been at Camp Shelby for about a month and a half. I was sitting in my bunk area cleaning my rifle and Kriesel burst through the door, butt-ass naked except for a gas mask, shrieking: "Gas! Gas! Gas!" He grabbed someone (I think it was Micheletti) and started shaking him. "Why aren't you putting your gas mask on? This is serious!" Kriesel ran around naked so much that by the time we left Shelby, I was more familiar with his junk than I was with my own.

"Do you guys need any help?" Kriesel asked the working Seabees.

"Oh come on," one of the Seabees replied. Kriesel stood below them completely naked with a towel draped over his shoulder, holding his hygiene kit.

"If you need a hand, I'll be in the shower, so just let me know."

"Oh, for Christ's sake," the Seabee said.

"Dude," another Seabee said, "that thing ain't as impressive as you seem to think it is." In truth his unit was probably bigger than most guys', but nobody wanted to encourage him. A day seldom went by without Kriesel talking about how big his dork was, and if he'd known that we sort of agreed with him, he wouldn't have put on a pair of pants for the entire deployment.

Not being blessed with the massive man-meat that Kriesel packed, I resorted to recreational drug use to help alleviate the boredom and monotony of life at the pump house. As part of its antismoking campaign, the military gave out antidepressants to help curb nicotine cravings. They gave us sixty pills at a time and told us to come back if we ran out.

I've never smoked cigarettes, but I didn't want to turn down free drugs, so I told the military doctor that I was having trouble quitting. A bunch of other guys "quit" smoking too, but for the sake of their military careers I won't mention them by name. After a lot of careful research, we found that eight pills was just the right amount to fuck us up for about three hours.

Like me, Yogi indulged in our government-supplied pharmaceuticals for entertainment. "Hey Maurstad," Yogi said in his thick Uzbek accent, "will you take some of these pills with me tonight? I don't want to be the only one tripping balls."

Me on the roof with a couple of Seabees trying to escape Kriesel's nakedness.

"Yeah man, I'm definitely up for that. I don't have any of my own, though."

"All right, you can have some of these." He handed me the anti-depressants and I swallowed them with a bunch of water.

It took a few hours for them to kick in, but once they corrupted the chemicals in my brainpan, I felt like I was one hundred feet tall. I found it nearly impossible to deal with the wind at that altitude.

To escape the wind I went into the tower that Token occupied. I sat and talked to him about how happy I was and how wonderful the world was. I said crazy things like "Iraq isn't such a bad place," and "I really like this part of the world," and "maybe when the war is over I'll move here."

149

The entire squad helped build the UFC ring for the fight.

Token grew tired of the nonsense coming out of my mouth, so he kicked me out of his tower. I walked around for a while longer until I found the food storage room. There I found a stash of chocolate Otis Spunkmeyer muffins, a crucial part of the pump house diet.

After eating about fifteen of the muffins I sat by myself while I came down off of the drugs. I became very depressed as my brain overcompensated for the antidepressants.

"Hey, you should kill yourself," a little voice in my head advised.

"I don't want to kill myself," I replied. "Why would I do that?"

"Think about it. It's a good idea. Kill yourself."

My brain had a point. "Maybe I should kill myself." This argument went on for a few minutes and fortunately the suicidal thoughts didn't prevail. I passed out shortly after I decided not to suck-start my rifle.

Meanwhile, Kriesel found Yogi on the roof crying. "Hey man, are you okay?"

Rolling over after one of Corey's wake-up calls.

"Yeah, I'm fine," Yogi sobbed.

"You know, you can talk to me if you need to. I understand what you are going through. Talking about things helps. I know I have a hard time dealing with being here sometimes too."

"No, you don't understand."

"I do understand, Yogi. All of us have a tough time with this sometimes."

"No, you don't. Just leave me alone."

"All right, if that is what you want. I'll be downstairs if you need anything."

What Kriesel didn't understand was that Yogi was dealing with being in Iraq just fine. He was just really fucked up and coming down from the antidepressants.

The next day, Rystad woke me up. The manner in which he did this (he woke me up almost daily in the same fashion) perplexes me to this day. It always began with a light shaking of the mattress and a quiet calling of my

I struggle to save my sandwich while Dunna and Nelly tape me to a chair.

name. (I know this because I was already awake one time, wanting to see just how he went about it.) I had slept through gunfire, so there was no way that this method of shaking the mattress would have roused me.

From the mattress shake, it progressed immediately to five or six hard jabs to the rib cage. Though this did accomplish the desired effect of getting my ass moving, I invariably started my day in a less than ideal mood.

"What the fuck is wrong with you!" I snapped at Corey. "Why can't you just wake me up without hurting me?"

"I tried but you didn't wake up."

"Jesus Christ! All you need to do is shake my shoulder and tell me to get up. I can't stand it when you jab me in the ribs like that."

"Well, if you'd wake up, I wouldn't do that."

Frustrated with my friend, I gave up the argument and got ready for my tower shift.

I manage to escape the room still attached to the chair, only to fall down and receive more tape.

When I got into my tower, Rystad was milling around on the ground below. Thinking it would be a funny prank, I walked out onto the catwalk between the two buildings our towers sat on and dumped a bottle of water on him as he passed below. Despite the relatively warm temperatures that day and the cool refreshingness of the water, he was not pleased with the prank.

He turned fiery red and ran up the stairs, the water seeming to boil off of his skin. He met me at the end of the catwalk where it joined the stairs and the roof. He pushed me, wanting to fight, and I struggled to catch myself because there weren't yet railings on either the catwalk or the stairs.

When I got my balance I put my hand on Rystad's shoulder and tried to calm him down so that we wouldn't fight on a three-foot wide catwalk fifteen feet up in the air. I talked him out of his rage, and once he was calmed down, he took a step back onto the top step of the stairs. When his foot came down,

Our lavish Thanksgiving feast.

Celebrating the holiday together. We became as close as any family, and we fought as much as any family.

the step broke and he fell backward, sliding on his back all the way down the steps, nearly falling off. When he got to the bottom, he stood up, obviously in pain, his eyes filled with more rage than before.

"You fucking pushed me!" he yelled, ready to charge.

"The step broke," I argued with him. "I didn't push you." Corey would have none of it. He was ready to charge up the stairs and tackle me off the catwalk, knocking us both to our certain doom.

He must have realized that charging me would result in both our deaths. Instead he decided to get Nelly to help him set up an Ultimate Fighting Championship (UFC) ring for us to have a sanctioned and regulated fight. I was relieved from my tower shift about twenty minutes early to fight a fight

156

that I really had no interest in fighting, especially since it was against one of my best buddies.

"In this corner, weighing in at one hundred and seventy-five pounds, we have Corey 'Airborne' Rystad!" Nelly shouted the introduction at the camera being operated by Dunna, who was sitting on a pile of sandbags, giggling.

"In the other corner, weighing in at one hundred and eighty-five pounds and ugly as fuck, Nick 'the Pan Man' Maurstad." The nickname had evolved over time and I was even given a theme song to go along with it by Gib Trontvet:

Pan, Pan, Greek god Pan
One part goat, the other part man.

Trontvet wasn't a man given to spontaneous bursts of song, but he did like to give everyone a hard time and put a great deal of effort into his practical jokes. He was the ringleader of a caper to desecrate Adam Seed's bed. Seed was obsessive-compulsive about his bed—he wigged out if anyone even touched it—so one day Trontvet took sexy nude photos of a bunch of guys laying on Seed's bed. He downloaded the photos, which showed every square inch of Seed's bed covered in sweaty man ass, onto Seed's computer for him to discover. Seed tried to get Trontvet back by pulling an even more extravagant practical joke involving a slam pig (for those of you over a certain age, a slam pig is a woman with whom you might fornicate if enough alcohol is involved, but you certainly wouldn't want anyone to discover your indiscretion) that Trontvet hosed while home on leave and a falsified pregnancy test. Seed lacked Trontvet's panache, though, and wasn't able to pull the caper off. All in all, I was glad to just be the subject of Trontvet's little Pan song.

"I want a good clean fight," Nelly said, bringing us both into the middle of the ring. "I don't want to see any punches to the face or any of this," he said, hitting us both in the nuts.

"What the fuck man?" I complained. "Why would you do that?"

Corey, on the other hand, was unfazed. He was so pumped up and into the fight that he didn't even notice getting hit in the balls. This didn't bode well for me. He was stone cold and ready to kick my ass.

The fight started and, after a couple of seconds waiting for Corey to make a move, I went in to throw him on the ground. I tried to trip him backward but he blocked me. Though my first attempt to get him down failed, I did manage to accidentally face plant him. This turned the fight into a grappling affair on the

157

Nelly and Dunna help with some construction.

ground. For the next two or three minutes we enacted a semi-public display of some of the worst fighting technique ever, performing an interpretive dance of UFC ineptitude inside that plywood ring in rural Fallujah. When we reviewed the videotape after the fight, we realized I'd invented a new fighting style, which we named "the pistons." This consisted of rapid piston-like punches to Corey's torso that did little more than annoy him.

Eventually, we worked our way into a mutual choke hold that, on the videotape Dunna made, didn't look like any form of hand-to-hand combat that any of us had ever seen. Instead it looked more like a trailer for a film called *Brokeback Pump House*. We each had the other by the neck in some fashion and were both being choked. Seconds before I was about to submit to Corey's choke, he tapped my arm signaling his defeat.

The fight seemed to let out a lot of the frustration between Corey and me, frustration that had built up from living together in such tight quarters for so long. After the fight, we got along much better and our friendship returned to the level it had been early in our deployment. We started spending time quoting senseless lines from the movie *Wayne's World* and making fun of Horn together again.

Two days later, it was Thanksgiving. Morale was a bit low because we knew that everyone on base was enjoying a nice, hot Thanksgiving meal with turkey, stuffing, potatoes, ham, and anything else usually found on the standard American Thanksgiving table. Meanwhile, we were eating MREs, Otis Spunkmeyer muffins, Lay's Arabic potato chips, and drinking powder mix Gatorade.

In the late afternoon, Eve showed up with a couple of Bradleys and a supply of sliced turkey, ham, and roast beef with a few bags of buns. We set up a fifteen-foot table with a mighty feast of sliced meats, buns, Otis Spunkmeyer muffins, potato chips, and Arabic Mountain Dew, which always tasted a little odd to me. It tasted a little like the Iraqis from Anbar Province smelled—sickly sweet and perfumed, with a slight undercurrent of feces. It was the perfect complement to Lay's Arabic potato chips and MREs.

That night the squad sat down as a family. We stretched the meal out, rotating our work schedule so the guys in the towers could come in and eat with the rest of us, and ate Thanksgiving dinner.

The next day I was watching *He-Man and the Masters of the Universe* on DVD with Dunna, Nelly, and Corporal Chris Ness. Ness joined our squad as a supplement along with Lance Corporal Miller. The other guys were all in their beds while I sat in the middle of the room in a chair.

I was enjoying a roast beef sandwich and a Coke, when Dunna jumped up out of bed with a roll of duct tape and tried to tape me to the chair. I thwarted the mischief and sent the defeated troublemaker on his way.

I got back into the roast beefy goodness of my sandwich and was paying close attention to the way Battle Cat morphed from a cowardly green tiger into a godless killing machine, when Dunna snuck up from behind. The sneaky little bastard had enlisted the help of Nelly. I was overpowered and despite my best efforts I was unable to fend off the attack.

LEFT: Specialist Damien Kohler joined our squad while I was on leave. He spent most of his time being an old (27), surly chain smoker. RIGHT: Corporal Chris Ness also joined our squad while I was on leave. He spent his free time taking most of the pictures in this book.

The next five minutes were spent using the entire roll of duct tape to attach me securely to the chair. After an epic struggle I managed to escape my oppressors. I hobbled out of the room using the one leg that wasn't attached to the chair and left my sandwich behind. By this time it had been stepped on and ruined anyway.

I charged out of the room, destroying the cheap chair as I went through the doorway, and found Grub and Kohler standing outside laughing at me. Specialist Damien Kohler was a truck driver sent to us from the mechanics in a one-for-one trade for the disgraced Neumiller. The mechanics definitely got the stinky end of that stick.

Grub and Kohler produced a second roll of tape and taped me to the tattered remnants of the chair. Once again I fought a valiant struggle in an attempt to throw off the shackles of my oppressors, but I was no match for them. I gave up halfway through the roll and they continued taping me to the

160

chair until they lost interest and left me for dead, lying on the ground taped to the chair.

When Grub decided that I looked sufficiently pathetic writhing around in a big mess of duct tape and broken chair and begging to be set free, he cut me loose with a pair of medical scissors. I began plotting how to get my revenge, careful not to raise the stakes so high that the next round of retaliation would be unbearable. The events that would unfold over the next week would prevent me from ever carrying out whatever plans I devised.

CHAPTER 18:
December 2, 2006

I N THE WEE HOURS OF DECEMBER 2, 2006, I lay in the stairway of a house we had occupied the morning before, writing a letter to a friend of mine. I hunkered down in my sleeping bag, my headlamp illuminating my small notebook, cursing the other half of my squad. After being discovered by a group of children, they left their OP early and walked back to Camp Fallujah to get a hot meal and sleep in their warm beds, leaving us to suffer the cold December night with nothing to eat but MREs.

I wrote my friend a letter detailing the events of the two months since I had last seen her when I was back in Minnesota on leave. I wrote about my roommates, my leaders, and the chow. I kept the details about what was happening in Iraq brief:

> Since I returned from leave, things here have gotten a bit crazy. It's completely opposite of the boredom I faced before I went home for leave. Since I returned, someone in my company has been shot at about two or three times a month and in the last two weeks my platoon alone has hit four IEDs and found an additional thirty-two. It's a rare day when my company doesn't find an IED and a rare week that someone isn't blown up. Thankfully no one has died yet but there have been a bunch of people hurt.

I concluded the letter and crawled further into my sleeping bag in a largely failed attempt to escape the cold. I needed to get some rest before I took another shift watching the area for suspicious activity.

Alpha Team with Nelly on the morning of December 2, 2006.

I was awakened for my shift at 0900 and watched the village and the mosque across the canal. I spent my shift talking to the naval corpsman assigned to our squad. We called Hospital Corpsman Third Class Michael Wells "Doc," just like every other medic in our unit. He worked in the aid station on base until he volunteered to start working with us.

For the second day in a row, Alpha team couldn't find a suitable site to set up its OP before the sun came up. This wasn't the team's fault, but that didn't stop us from standing on our roof cursing them for having a short day.

Every morning at 0500 the mosque at checkpoint 36 broadcast morning prayers, around 1300 it broadcast midday prayers, and at sunset it broadcast the evening prayers. Some dude with a voice that sounded like the braying of a horny coyote sang these prayers. That afternoon the speakers came to life about halfway between the afternoon prayers and evening prayers, only instead of the singer yodeling out his prayers, a man started speaking in Arabic.

"What the hell is he saying?" I asked Dave, our translator.

"He's from the mujahedeen," Dave said. "He's talking about killing the American infidels."

After my shift, I went back into the house to eat the barely palatable beef stew MRE and get a little bit more sleep before we walked back to Flanders. Late that afternoon Horn woke me up with a slight kick in the leg and told me we needed to get packed and ready to go so we wouldn't have to spend fifteen minutes getting our shit together when it was time to leave.

When I was finished packing I went outside to relax in the cool December evening. It wasn't long before we noticed two cobra helicopters circling and one CH-46 landing about two miles away. It was a medevac. None of us had heard the explosion from an IED that ripped through a humvee less than twenty minutes earlier.

No one in Bravo team had any inkling that our brothers were in trouble. Our radio was on a different station, none of us heard the explosion, we didn't see a cloud of smoke, and there was no way for us to know anything was wrong. As far as we knew, Alpha team was probably taking a late afternoon nap at Flanders waiting for us to get back so we could all go back to Camp Fallujah.

Later, Horn theorized that God must have shielded us from knowing anything until we were in a safe place, but his idea that some magical friend in the sky would protect half of our squad while letting the other half get blown into smithereens seemed completely ludicrous to me.

After watching the helicopters for a while, we saw an EOD convoy drive past in the direction of the helicopters. They had a wrecker truck in the convoy, so we figured that someone had been blown up, which was such a common occurrence that we didn't give it much thought. Rarely had a soldier been injured badly enough to be sent away for medical treatment, and no one in our area had died from IEDs yet.

"We should head back and see what's going on," Horn said. After seeing all of the EOD vehicles and the wrecker drive by, Horn decided that we should leave our OP and see what the commotion was about. We'd already packed up most of our gear, so it only took us five minutes to put it on and step off on our hike back to Flanders. It was about a mile back, so we were there in less than fifteen minutes. We walked in, looking forward to relaxing and not doing any work for a few hours. I was the last guy to enter the pump house compound. On my way to the table where we stored our gear, Joe Ness stopped me. Ness was one of the nicest guys I'd ever met, but no one should ever have to suffer receiving any bad news from him. His shitty delivery lacked an iota of tact or comfort.

He stood between me and a railing, looking more upset than I'd ever seen him. "Have you heard the news?"

"No. What the fuck are you talking about?" I was angry that whatever he had to say couldn't wait until I wasn't weighed down with body armor and a heavy backpack with a radio in it.

"McDonough is KIA, dude."

I was way too tired for a sick joke like this. "I am going to get my gear off and kick your ass." I hit the rail between us for emphasis. "That shit isn't fucking cool to joke about!"

"I am not joking, man." Ness said, backing away.

Lieutenant Mike Casey, the company executive officer, came out of the small building behind Ness and told me to go get my gear off; then he went to round up everyone to make sure we all got the information at the same time.

I stumbled back and walked over to the table, trying to comprehend what I had just heard. The last ninety seconds had been too much to process; the flood of thoughts and emotions were too complex to get my head around in such a short time. Grub asked me what was going on. I couldn't do anything but mumble a couple of words and point him toward Casey. He somehow understood, and Casey rounded everyone up for a talk.

I sat on the ground with a couple of the guys, while a few others stood behind us and waited for the news. I was staring at the nothingness two inches in front of my face; everything else was out of focus. Casey started talking. "About two hours ago, Specialist McDunno . . . Mc . . . Mc . . . Mc . . ." Casey stammered, looking at Ness to see if he had gotten the name right. "Mc . . . Donough [he finally pronounced the name right: 'McDunna'], is it? Spec. McDonough was killed by an IED about two hours ago at checkpoint thirty-four. Specialist Rystad is also not doing very well. We don't know if he will make it. Sergeant Kriesel may lose his legs and Staff Sergeant Nelson may

Dunna and Rystad sit in OP on December 2, 2006

have broken his back. Lance Corporal Miller appears to be doing just fine. I am sure you are all going to want to talk about this, so if you need anything from me, just ask. I'll be inside that door." He pointed to the building behind him. Whenever something bad happened, Casey mouthed platitudes about "being there for us if we needed anything." Most of our officers really would have been there for us, men like Lieutenant Blomgren and Captain Rankin, but Casey would have just mouthed more platitudes had we sought his help.

Horn stood up and asked everyone to go sit down in the gym for a talk. We gathered around sitting on various pieces of exercise equipment or the floor. "I would like to say a few things for Bryan in a prayer. Maurstad, I know you don't necessarily believe in God or any of that sort of thing, but maybe if you

Kriesel and Dunna, ready to fire.

don't mind . . ."

"Dude, it's fine. Just say what you are going to say."

"Okay. If anyone wants to add anything when I am done, feel free." Horn paused, then said, "Please guide Bryan on his journey to his final resting place so that we will one day see him again. Lord, watch over John, Corey, Tim, and Bruce. Help them to heal and make it through their injuries. And finally, God, watch over us so that we may carry on the mission without them."

He finished talking and no one else spoke much, at least not that any of us remember. The next forty-five minutes seems to be a black spot in our collective memory, and no one recalled exactly what happened. Horn remembered that we talked about Corey and how we hoped he would make it. There were a

On the roof ready to go back to Flanders.

few attempts at humor to lighten the mood, but like the rest of us, he didn't remember any details. All I remember was staring at the floor until Horn called in on the radio to find us a ride back to Camp Fallujah.

He was told that we would just have to wait a little bit, because no one was ready to come and get us. Horn started arguing with the radio operator until Captain Rankin got on the radio and told him that there was no one to come out and get us, so the best thing to do was to calm down and prepare to spend a few more hours at the pump house.

"Do you know who the fuck is out here? That is our squad that got hit today and we need to be in with our boys right fucking now!" Horn yelled into the radio at the commander.

Colonel Bristol took the radio from Captain Rankin: "Horn, this is Hammer Six and, if I have to come out there myself, you and your men will be back on base within the hour."

What's left of the humvee.

Just as Colonel Bristol had promised, an escort picked us up within the hour. Horn, Grub, Yogi, and Kohler took the humvee we'd driven out there two days earlier, while I got into Sergeant Hernandez's Bradley with Doc Wells, Dave the 'terp, and Corporal Ness. It was a short, quiet ride back to base. We stopped just inside the gate, cleared our weapons as usual, and then continued on to our compound. We stopped on the road in front of our compound and the ramp in the back of the Bradley dropped. I stood up and walked out. My teary-eyed platoon sergeant greeted me with a big hug. Someone took my rifle and Token took my body armor vest and my leg pouch.

Jake Brown and Brian Micheletti, two of McDonough's best friends, both gave me a hug and told me that if I needed anything to let them know. The rest of the platoon was just a few feet off the road. We all stood around hugging each other and talking.

Lieutenant Blomgren asked everyone to quiet down. He told us that the latest word from Camp Taqaddum was that Rystad had died en route to the

The hole left by the blast was about seven feet across and four feet deep.

hospital. Kriesel was in very bad shape and they didn't know if he would make it. They didn't know much about Nelson's injuries yet, but he was doing well. Miller had only minor injuries and would likely be coming back eventually. Blomgren also told us that we would be able to go pay our last respects to Dunna before seeing him off later that night.

The platoon stayed in a close group for about ten minutes in the front of the company motor pool, and we talked amongst each other. Some were crying, some were filled with hate, and some were too shocked to have any reaction at all, but all of us were trying to comfort each other after the loss of two of our brothers. I couldn't function properly anymore and just wandered around aimlessly trying to make sense of it all.

After a few minutes we began to trickle back to our barracks. I walked near the back of the group, my arm around Winnie, the two of us talking about how we couldn't believe that Corey and Dunna were gone.

About half the platoon stayed outside on the smoking porch behind our barracks. Almost everyone was smoking, even people who didn't smoke. I managed to refrain from lighting up but stayed out with everyone anyway. I didn't feel like talking about anything but I didn't want to be anywhere by myself.

Later the platoon made its way over to the tent in which they were going to put Dunna's body. We huddled outside while two marines, one on each end of a stretcher, carried Dunna's body, which was inside a black body bag, out of one tent and into the other. When I saw Dunna on the stretcher, everything finally became clear to me and I started crying.

We were invited inside once everything was situated. A marine chaplain stood at one end of the table with Lieutenant Blomgren. First Sergeant Eggert directed people in. I was told to go in front by the table with the rest of my squad and Dunna's closest friends.

The chaplain said some Catholic prayers for Dunna and then some prayers for Corey. He told all of us that we could put our hand on the foot end of the bag and have a quiet moment with Dunna before we left the tent. No one moved or said anything for a couple of minutes, and then people started to walk up and pay their last respects to our fallen brother on the table.

I waited until most of the others had gone past Dunna to take my turn, wanting to be with my friend as long as possible. I walked to the end of the table, put my hand on the end of the bag, felt the toe of Dunna's boot through the black PVC material, and watched a couple of tears fall to the ground. *I'm going to miss you, Bryan,* I thought. *Goodbye, buddy.* I looked back up, turned around, and left the tent.

When I got outside, I sat down and leaned against a shipping container. I wasn't ready to go back to the barracks. Neither was anyone else, and when everyone finished saying goodbye to Corey, we all stood around outside the tent, not saying a word. After a few minutes a marine amphibious assault vehicle (AAV) drove up next to Fallujah Surgical, the surgery hospital where they sent people who were really fucked up and were picked up by ambulance. People who got fucked up and were picked up by helicopter went to TQ, where they had better surgical care. They'd hauled Kriesel to TQ, where five surgeons worked on him for hours, barely saving his life.

Walking back to Flanders.

More AAVs came screaming up to Fallujah Surgical and a bunch of marines jumped out, yelling like crazy. Some people in scrubs ran out, unloaded two stretchers, and brought them inside. Another marine helped his buddy limp into the hospital and the AAV drove off.

We watched this take place in complete silence, and then we all walked to the chow hall to eat as a platoon. It was almost midnight and we wouldn't be sending Dunna off in the chopper until 0200. We took up a corner of the chow hall and ate as a family. We tried to lighten the mood by telling a few jokes and funny stories about Dunna and Corey, but were all still worrying about Kriesel.

When we got back to our barracks I was in my room with Grub and Winnie, talking about Corey and how it just didn't seem like he was really gone. We all felt like he would walk through the door at any moment. His bed looked the way it always did—the blankets thrown toward the wall, his DVD player in the place where normal people put their pillows, and his pillow in the corner. The headphones that were still connected to the player dangled off the edge of the bed and his *Everybody Loves Raymond* disc was still in the player.

Sergeant Rogers came into our room to check on us. "Hey guys, how are you doing?"

"I think we are doing okay, considering," Winnie replied.

"Yeah, yeah, I understand," our platoon sergeant continued. "Listen, I hate to ask you guys this right now, but do you think that you could get all of Corey's stuff put onto his bed. We have to get it shipped out to his parents by tomorrow afternoon and I just want to make sure we get it all. I don't want to be in here trying to guess what belonged to him and what belongs to the three of you."

"Yeah, I think we can do that for you," I said. "Hey Rog, are you doing okay?"

He got a little choked up. "Yeah, I am doing all right. Thanks for asking."

After Sergeant Rogers left we got busy trying to get all of Corey's stuff together before going to the helicopter pad to see Dunna off. We started to go through all of his things and stack them on his bed. We tried to lighten the situation with some humor, making lame jokes like: "I think we better keep all of his jerky. Corey would have wanted it that way." We got all of his stuff picked up in about an hour, just in time to leave for the helo-pad.

When we arrived the whole company formed two lines, making a gauntlet through which they would carry Dunna, letting us see him one last time on his way to the CH-47 that would take him on the first leg of his journey home. The ambulance arrived just a couple of minutes before the helicopters landed. Micheletti, Brown, Gallagher, and Sergeant Matthew Pietrzak carried Dunna through the two lines of soldiers. Everyone dropped their salute as he passed them. The four-man detail put Dunna in one of the choppers and everyone raised one last salute. The first chopper took off and flew away, while the one carrying Dunna hovered for a minute in front of us before speeding off into the dark night sky, taking our friend home.

174

December 2, 2006

I walked back to my barracks and went to bed to rest up for work the next day. I might have just lost two of my best friends, but we still had a job to do when the sun came up. I was right back out in the same area the very next morning.

CHAPTER 19:
Memorial

THE DAY AFTER COREY AND DUNNA DIED, Captain Rankin came up to Horn and said, "Hey Horn, I hate to ask you and your guys to do this, but I have to have you out there today because we don't have the manpower to run the roadblocks unless you guys get out there on QRF. I'm sorry. You can have the next day off."

"I'll have my guys ready," Horn replied.

We got ready and went out to the mosque that I'd flown over with the Raven. Most of the rest of the company was setting up roadblocks in response to the IED. They blocked off every road and made everyone coming into or leaving the area enter or exit on a single road. We hung back, waiting for someone to be attacked, in which case we'd respond. We were in exactly the right frame of mind to be on QRF because you want the quick reaction force to be staffed with the meanest, angriest motherfuckers available. After losing our friends, we were all that and more.

The squad consisted of everyone who hadn't been blown up the day before—Grub, Horn, Ness, Yogi, Kohler, and me—along with Micheletti, Winnie, and Gallagher, who were assigned to our squad to replace Kriesel, Rystad, and Dunna, as well as Nelly and Miller. Nelly had been pretty banged up in the explosion and was out of action for a couple of weeks. Miller got fucked up worse than we'd originally been led to believe. He tore up the triceps muscles in his right arm and had some bleeding on his brain. They sent him to Germany and he never came back to Iraq.

We got a call from the operations center telling us that some Iraqis were hanging around the crater where the humvees had gotten blown up. We drove down there for a look around. There was no one there. We got out and looked at the pit for a few minutes, none of us saying anything. I felt overwhelmed, standing over the six-foot-deep pit. The EOD investigators said that the IED consisted of two one-hundred-pound propane tanks on top of two hundred pounds of explosives. All that was left of the humvee was tiny chips of metal, none more than two inches across. A QRF squad had removed all the bigger pieces of the vehicle.

Some shrubby little plants grew in the gravel around the area, and they were covered with some kind of brown spray. I realized it was blood.

"Let's get out of here," Horn said. "I can't look at this shit anymore." We turned around and went back to the mosque.

We wanted to tear that fucking mosque down. We kept thinking about the son-of-a-camel-fucker who urged the killing of Americans from the mosque the day before, and we wanted to go into that mosque and shoot everything that moved. But we couldn't do anything to the mosque. We tried to call in an artillery strike on it once, for no particular reason other than we just wanted to see it and everything inside of it blown straight to hell, but Horn wouldn't allow us to blow it up. In retrospect he probably made the right decision. Still, our inability to attack the people who had urged the killing of our friends frustrated us and fueled our rage. The only way we could shoot at a mosque was if people were shooting at us from inside. If people outside the mosque shot at us, then ran inside, the best we could do was call an Iraqi army unit and hope they'd show up, then hope that they'd pursue the bad guys into the mosque. Just getting someone back at base to call in an Iraqi unit was the hardest part. Finding some POG cocksucker on base willing to pull his head out of his ass long enough to figure out how to contact the Iraqi army was damn near impossible.

When it got dark we went home, not having accomplished anything when it came to finding the men who'd murdered our friends. We spent the next couple of days talking with chaplains and counselors. By the end of the two days Winnie, Grub, and I could no longer stand to look at Corey's empty top bunk, so we dismantled it and Frankensteined the remaining bunk onto the two bunks on the opposite side of the room, so we had one three-tiered bunk bed.

The Shrine set up to honor Bryan and Corey during the memorial service held in the chapel at Camp Fallujah.

It eventually turned out to be sort of awkward because we had developed an unspoken policy of allowing in-room masturbation, as long as it wasn't too obvious. We indulged each other in this so we didn't have to go whack off in the stinking porta-shitters. We had curtains around our bunks so no one had to see us jerking it, but when we got three full-sized males slapping the salami on a tall, three-tiered bunk bed all at the same time, it got a little unstable. We came close to tipping over the entire unit once or twice.

For the next few days, I kept seeing Corey walking around base with me. Almost every time I turned around I saw him walking away from me or ducking behind a corner. I tried to catch him, but whenever I turned whatever corner he had gone around, I found nothing. I shed a tear or two and resumed whatever it was that I had been doing before I started chasing ghosts.

Nelly returned to Fallujah a few days later. It was around eight in the morning when he walked into my room. He walked up to our three-tiered

Ecker and Slater put a magnetic cross shaped like the tattoo on Bryan's arm on the side of their humvee.

bunk, telling us how happy he was to see us, trying his hardest to fight back his tears. He gave me a big hug.

"I'm glad you're okay," I said through my tears. By then everyone in the room was crying. We sat teary eyed and talked with Nelly about how Kriesel and Miller were doing.

The day after Nelly returned, we had a memorial service for Dunna and Corey. We had just resumed our normal patrol work, though I didn't feel very good about being back on the roads that had claimed the lives of our friends.

Someone had put up a large tribute to our fallen brothers in the front of the chapel. A large picture of Corey stood at one side of the tribute and a large picture of Dunna at the other side. A table under each picture held the medals, coins, and awards each of them had earned in the military. Between the pictures and tables were the company and battalion guidon flags, the

U.S. Marine Corps flag, and the American flag. Below the flags sat a pair of upside-down rifles, a helmet covering each. A pair of boots and dog tags—the traditional memorials for those killed in the line of duty—rested beneath each rifle.

When I walked into the chapel I saw a bunch of generals who I didn't know. At the end of the row of nondescript generals, I saw the Elicerio. I hadn't seen the Elicerio since Camp Shelby. It took eight months and two deaths to make him finally set foot in Fallujah.

Sergeant Dillon Jennings, one of our radio technicians, made a slideshow video for both Dunna and Corey. The videos were just a couple of songs with pictures and video footage of each of them. After the videos Colonel Bristol, Lieutenant Colonel Parks, Captain Rankin, and Lieutenant Blomgren all gave short eulogies. Parks did seem to genuinely care that two of his soldiers had died, but unlike Bristol, Rankin, and Blomgren, he wouldn't have been able to pick either one out of a crowd.

After the officers spoke, the chaplain read a few bible verses, and Dunna and Corey's friends started speaking. When my turn came, I took out some notes I'd made, and read:

> When I started writing this, I sat and stared at a blank page for the better part of three hours. Writing all of this makes the whole thing seem more like reality instead of the bad dream or awful mistake I want it to be. It reminds me that Corey isn't really going to walk through the door any minute, like he had just been to chow or talking on the phone.
>
> Not having Corey here has driven home what great a guy my friend really was. How down to earth and real he was. How he was always laughing and smiling, even when it was completely unreasonable for him to be happy. That is what I will always remember about Corey.
>
> It always brightened my day to look over and see Corey's face beaming after he had received a package with a new magazine or recorded hockey game to watch. He'd get excited just from opening an MRE and finding some strawberry jam.
>
> "Yeah! I got some strawberry jam! Woo hoo!" It was almost ridiculous how something so small could make Corey's day so good.

I also know that if no one would have laughed at that story, Corey would have been the first person to turn and look at me, with a perfectly straight face, and say, "Crickets, Maurstad. Crickets."

While Corey was always quick to criticize my bad jokes, he also laughed the hardest at my good ones. I memorized a few monologues from *Wayne's World 2*, and every time I would recite them, Corey's face would get so beet red that I would have to stop. He would laugh so hard that I sometimes worried he had stopped breathing.

Corey was quick to share anything he had gotten in a care package. Most recently he was handing out venison jerky his parents had sent him. For the first few days it was some of the best I had ever eaten, but, as it got older, the jerky began to mold. And there was Corey, still giving it away. When I expressed my concern that he was eating moldy food, he assured me that it was perfectly fine if you scraped off the mold with your fingernail.

I loved Corey like a brother and I am glad to have had the opportunity to honor him and share some of the experiences I had with him. Corey, I love you and I miss you.

After the memorial was over, those of us who spoke at the memorial got in a line at the door to greet everyone as they left. Most guys gave me and the other guys in line a hug as they passed by. Toward the end of the line, Corporal Sorano—a short female Hispanic marine with a ginormous rack who was part of Bristol's entourage—came by to shake Everson's hand. Everson was the first person in line, and he pulled Corporal Sorano to him and gave her a big hug. This set the standard, so Sorano hugged everyone as she went down the line. It felt great to get a hug from a beautiful woman with massive milk bags after not having touched female flesh for months.

Outside the chapel, when we were standing around shooting the shit, Bristol said, "It was great hugging you guys in there, but when Corporal Sorano gave me a hug, that really boosted my morale." He started to walk away, but looked back over his shoulder and said, "And that, gentlemen, is why I'll never be a general."

A couple of weeks after the memorial, the Elicerio came out to see Pump House Flanders with his penis-headed Sergeant Major Douglas Julin. Julin, who

Sergeant Major Shit Sandwich.

looked like a cross-eyed version of Major Frank Burns from the old *M*A*S*H* TV show, was the pompous assbag proxy of the Elicerio. Julin followed the Elicerio around like stink follows a dog with infected anal glands.

No one is really sure what happened next, but Bravo company folklore holds that Bristol was seriously disturbed about the Elicerio being in his AO. One account has Bristol roundhouse kicking two-by-fours in half, while another account has him making balloon animals with one-inch cast-iron pipe. Both accounts place Thorn in a tower just above Bristol, cowering in the corner with his Ka-bar knife clutched tightly to his chest. He was worried Bristol would go into a white Berserker-like rage, killing friend and foe alike.

Most accounts have the Elicerio telling O'Connell that he needed to get his colonel behind a desk where he belongs. This was about as wise a move as poking a sleeping grizzly bear in the balls with a twig. No one knows exactly what happened next, but most accounts agree it was ugly and ended with Julin weeping openly and the Elicerio soiling his uniform. Unconfirmed reports have Bristol telling the Elicerio, "Stay the fuck away from my soldiers. I will allow you to go to memorials, I will allow you to lay your coin down and pay your respects, and then I will allow you to leave without bothering any of my fucking men."

Whatever happened at the pump house that day, the Elicerio only came back to our AO once after that, and when he did, he was as quiet as a church mouse. From that day on Colonel Bristol was our real commander.

CHAPTER 20:
Operation Sledgehammer

N OT LONG AFTER THE MEMORIAL, marine Lance Corporal Jack Buda joined the squad to help fill in for Dunna and Corey. We'd been working extra hard since they'd been killed, and we needed all the help we could get.

Buda was the exotic-looking offspring of a Mexican man and a Polish woman. His dark Latino complexion contrasted with his strong Polack jaw and brow. He worked in the operation center as a radio operator before he joined us. The first time he ever left the base was going to be with us on Operation Sledgehammer. It looked like it was going to be a hell of a way to pop his cherry.

We spent the day before Operation Sledgehammer preparing our gear, reviewing the commander's intent for the large-scale mission, and going over our battle drills. Horn and I grilled Buda on battle drills because it would be his first time going outside the wire. "What do you do if we get shot at? What do you do if we have incoming?" Buda had it all down for the most part, but we wanted to make sure he understood everything. We told him to either stay right behind me or right behind Horn and he'd be all right.

Before the mission everyone lined up in the motor pool for our pre-mission checks. Our squad leaders and platoon sergeant looked over our gear, making sure we had packed everything that we'd need for the mission. While our platoon was doing this in our standard laidback and efficient style,

In a rare moment of calm, Corporal Chris Dean refrains from pointing his rifle at anyone.

2nd Platoon was stuck in a living hell administered by its platoon sergeant, Sergeant First Class Travis Manzke.

Manzke was a tall, skinny guy who walked so crow-footed he looked like Charlie Chaplin. He had lined up his entire platoon and was yelling at them because a couple of them didn't have their sleeping mats packed. We hadn't packed our sleeping mats, nor had most of the other soldiers and marines. The other platoon sergeants had sense enough to realize that packing lists were just guidelines and that we really didn't need our "puss pads" to accomplish this mission. While Manzke ragged on his men, we stood around laughing at them, enjoying the show their idiot platoon sergeant was putting on.

When Manzke finished his pointless bitching, Colonel Bristol gathered everyone together in the motor pool. "Men, I know we've lost some good men recently. When this happens, you have two groups of people—the ones who want to go out and kill everything they see and the ones who don't want to go out at all. You have to fight both those mindsets and just go out there and get the job done. I know you've been here a long time and that you're probably missing home right now, especially since it's hunting season," Colonel Bristol told the company. "Well, it's hunting season here, too. But we're hunting men. Let's go out there tomorrow and serve them up a big cold bowl of fuck!"

Operation Sledgehammer kicked off at 0700. The platoon met in the motor pool at 0600 to do a final check of our gear and vehicles to make sure that we had everything we needed to sustain us for two weeks in the field— MREs, three hundred rounds of 5.56 ammo, spare uniforms, fresh socks for every day we'd be outside the wire, extra t-shirts, and apparently a supply of bowls and several truckloads of cold fuck.

Once we were sure that everything was in order, we moved onto the pre-mission Kohler hump. This was a short-lived good-luck ritual in which a couple of us would give Kohler a vigorous humping before we left on a mission. Kohler didn't mind; in fact, he seemed to like it a little too much, which is why we soon abandoned the ritual.

We lined all of the vehicles up at the south gate, loaded our weapons, and did a last-minute review of the route we would be taking. We left camp a few minutes later and made the long, slow drive to the shit hole we would be raiding. After a few hours on the road at our typical six-mile-per-hour pace, we finally reached the hellish town of Zydon.

Zydon sits along the Euphrates River. It had been a safe haven for insurgents since the major operations in Fallujah drove them out of that town. Zydon has limited access because of the way the river winds around it. We called the peninsula of land underneath Zydon the "nut sack" because of its scrotum-like shape.

When we got to Zydon we started to raid the area one building at a time. The farther into the village we moved, the more resistance we encountered from the locals. They became uncooperative and flat out unruly. When the locals quit answering our questions, we started bringing them to the company firm base—the temporary base we used on operations, usually a school, a factory, or a really big house that we took over during the operation—to be questioned by the military interrogators. The interrogators were marines whose sole job was to interrogate people. This took place behind closed doors

Specialist Damien Kohler braces himself for the traditional pre-mission Kohler hump.

and I never saw any of them in action. Before they started, they'd tell us that we probably weren't going to like what we were about to see and suggested we leave, and I always left before the interrogation started.

As we went house to house, we picked up detainees, a couple here and a couple there. We took anyone who wouldn't cooperate with us and answer our questions. Dave, our 'terp, had a good sense of who was telling the truth and who was lying, and we detained anyone Dave identified as lying. We also detained people if we just had a bad feeling about them. Soon we had eight Iraqis in custody and it was getting to be a problem escorting them from house to house, so Horn charged me with escorting the detainees to the firm base. He sent Winnie along to help. We set out on our one-mile hike with eight Iraqis walking in line with their hands zip cuffed.

"Hey Maurstad," Winnie said from the back of the group, "what's with that box?"

Kohler gets humped by Grub and me. Only Grub humped to completion.

I hadn't noticed the box sitting in the road right in front of me, because the road was in a small trench and I was looking over the berms at the countryside, watching for people moving around, preparing for a possible attack. The box was at my feet by the time I saw it. With my next step, I would have stepped on the anal-bead trigger device sticking out of it.

"Holy fuck!" I yelled back to Winnie. "That's an IED! Let's get the fuck out of here!"

We took the detainees and ran two hundred meters away. Luckily, an EOD unit was passing by on the road. I got their attention and explained the situation to them. They drove over to it and dealt with it while Winnie and I continued on our hike with the detainees.

After we dropped the Iraqis off at the company firm base, we walked back to the area where our squad was working and resumed the building-to-building search, tearing apart houses and interrogating the occupants.

A soldier, who prefers not to be named, gets festive.

Eventually, we encountered resistance from the dogs in the area. They started out just growling and barking at us, but soon began following us around. I was walking in the rear of the group after we finished with a row of houses and two dogs were following at a distance.

When Micheletti and Winnie turned the corner, I was left alone with the dogs. They charged at me, growling and snarling as they ran. I jumped through a row of hedges and cut through a yard to catch up to Micheletti and Winnie. When I got to the other side of the yard, the dogs were closing in on me. I jumped through another row of bushes and found the guys on the other side.

"Kill the dogs!" I shouted as I jumped through bushes.

Micheletti turned to the bushes and shot the first dog as it jumped through after me. The shot scared the other dog off and we killed it while it ran through a field. And so began the great Fallujah dog massacre.

Alpha Company hit an IED and their Bradley burned to the ground.
Surprisingly, it was not due to incompetence.

After hearing about the attack, Lieutenant Blomgren instituted a dog
extermination policy in an effort to keep us safe. We were to kill any dog
that acted aggressively, in part to keep us from getting chased and bitten,
but it was also to allow quiet night insertion into villages. Before Blomgren
instituted canine genocide, the dogs would bark as soon as we walked into
a village at night, alerting everyone that we were there. Since we needed to
walk into a village undetected, our only option was to get rid of the dogs.
There were no Humane Society shelters nearby, so that meant resorting to
our M4s for the job.

When we'd just about cleared the entire AO of dogs, Captain Rankin drove
to the outskirts of Zydon to see what was out there. Rankin had Nelly come
with him and drive his humvee. It was Nelly's first mission since he came back
and Rankin wanted to keep an eye on him to make sure he was all right.

Lance Corporal Jack Buda, a Polish-Mexican marine, joined our squad just before Operation Sledgehammer.

Rankin, Nelly, Pratt, and a couple of marines arrived at the edge of the village in the humvee just after the Bradley that had been watching the area had left. The Bradleys leaving emboldened the insurgents, and they opened up on the humvee with machine guns and RPGs.

Rankin called up 3rd Squad leader Staff Sergeant Josh Hatton—an Anoka County, Minnesota, deputy whom we called "the Dirty Dep," because of his porn-star 'stache—and within a couple of minutes, Hatton and some members of his squad arrived in another humvee. They had barely stopped when an RPG just about took the head off of Specialist John Ecker, Hatton's machine gunner. The RPG didn't explode; instead, it became embedded in the wall of the building behind the humvee. Everyone bailed out of both humvees and took cover in an empty house.

While this was happening, our squad was walking along a ridge, shooting dogs and searching for weapons caches. We were about two kilometers away and could hear the shooting, but we couldn't tell which direction it was coming

Stacked in front of the door of a house, getting ready to raid it.

from, so we continued to search for weapons and shoot dogs, figuring that if someone needed us, they'd call us.

As we walked along the ridge, we heard artillery whistling through the air above our heads. It sounded like it was coming in on us. Winnie yelled, "Incoming!" and hit the dirt.

I turned around to see Buda staring wide-eyed, white-knuckling his rifle. "Buda!" I yelled. "Get down on that fucking berm!" I sat down next to him and we watched the artillery level the entire village. It was spectacular. Within minutes, the artillery had destroyed a village that was about the same size as my hometown. From watching the pattern of the 155mm rounds, I could tell that Pratt was giving the artillery unit coordinates to try to take out a mosque.

Horn, in a rare moment of productivity, helps pack the trunk of a humvee.

He walked rounds within a few hundred meters of the mosque when the artillery stopped.

Rankin and his men went a little ways into the destroyed village, but they didn't have to go far to realize that everything and everyone who had been outside was dead. There was carnage everywhere—dead cows, dead chickens, dead goats, dead sheep, dead people. The house from which the insurgents had been shooting was leveled. There was no possible way anyone could have survived inside of it. I bet they were surprised.

After that things got real quiet. We didn't encounter any more resistance.

The next afternoon Kohler pissed off Corporal Chris Dean, a marine who we regarded as an all-around douchebag. Ness and Kohler were lying on their sleeping bags on the ground, shooting a packet of MRE cheese back and

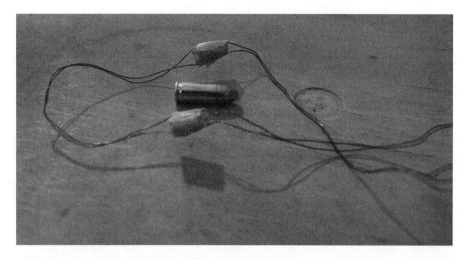

Anal bead trigger mechanism for an IED. *Minnesota National Guard*

forth with giant rubber exercise bands. They held the rubber bands with their feet and got some serious power into their shots. Kohler got the bright idea to shoot a cheese packet at Dean, who was sleeping. Kohler scored a direct cheese hit. Dean jumped up, pointed his gun at Kohler, and yelled, "I'm going to fucking kill you if you don't stop fucking with me! I'm just trying to get some goddamned sleep!" He stood over Kohler, who was still lying on his sleeping bag, trapped with nowhere to go.

Nelly, who had been watching the whole thing, was about to get up and kill Dean, but Ness diffused the whole situation. "Dean," he yelled, "put the fucking gun down!" Dean put the gun down and went back to sleep, like nothing had happened.

We tried to sleep after that, but an hour or two later, Blomgren came into the room. "Hey guys, listen up," he said, "I need four men with sons who can carry on their names to come with me right now. We've got some shit that needs to get done." In spite of his tempting offer, no one volunteered. We didn't know if Blomgren was serious or not, but we'd started to suspect that our lieutenant might be wearing his skivvies a size or two too tight. Lacking volunteers, he grabbed some guys and went out to clear a couple of houses. We never did find out if he was serious or joking, but since none of the guys who went out with him were killed it was a moot point.

Yogi questions a group of Iraqis.

We spent the next ten days pushing from house to house, working our way back to camp. While we were in Zydon kicking ass, our developmentally disabled sister company was in our normal AO trying to watch our ass. Alpha Company sat in our villages with its Bradleys, watching the roads and keeping anyone from coming down and attacking us from behind.

Our battalion commander, Lieutenant Colonel Spineless Six Parks, was in the same area as Alpha Company. He spent most of his time riding around in a humvee, trying to feel like an important part of the operation, even though he, like Alpha Company, was excluded from the real work in Zydon.

Early in the mission, Spineless Six found an IED and sat on the road in his humvee waiting for EOD to arrive and check it out. In the meantime, Everson rolled up in his Bradley.

"What's going on here?" Eve asked. "Why's the road blocked?"

"There is a possible IED in the road up there," Spineless Six replied.

"I don't see anything," Eve replied after scanning the road with the optics in the Bradley. He drove right past the lieutenant colonel and right over the IED that was there. In one fell swoop he made Parks look scared, worthless, and incompetent.

Somehow Alpha managed to fuck up even the simple task of keeping things quiet in our sector while we were out. They were successful in preventing any attacks on us, but in doing so they pissed off an entire village that had been friendly toward us for most of the deployment.

The story, as it was explained to us, was that a man carrying a white bag approached one of the Alpha Company Bradleys. Not knowing what to do, one member of Alpha fired a warning shot at the man. Not only was it unnecessary to fire the shot, but also in Anbar Province it's against the rules of engagement to fire warning shots at people. The only time a warning shot is authorized is on a vehicle.

The next problem with the warning shot was that the bungling shit-hook who fired the warning shot missed. He had the entire desert, hundreds of miles of empty gravel and sand to shoot at and all the fucktard had to do was not hit one little person in all of that emptiness. He failed.

I found out about it a few weeks later when the villagers got pissed off that the man had been shot. When they explained to us who it was that had been shot, I realized right away that I knew the guy.

Searching a field for weapons caches.

A few months earlier, Kriesel and I found the guy sitting by himself in a palm grove while we were doing a foot patrol of Namer. When we got close to him we noticed that there was something not quite right about him. He was sitting against the tree rocking back and forth, murmuring to himself.

"All right, Maurstad, go search him," Kriesel said to me. "I'll cover you."

"Are you serious?"

"Yeah, get over there and search him."

"Dude, he's fucking retarded."

"I don't care. We still need to search him."

"Fuck," I said, walking over to the guy who had a string of drool running down to a large wet spot on his man dress.

When I picked the guy up, he let out a moan and resisted, not like an insurgent, but like an unruly four-year-old kid who didn't want to be held by

Setting up our living quarters in an Iraqi house for a few days.

his mother when she tried to pick him up in a grocery store. Trying to hold this guy up and search him was nearly impossible, which made it all the more entertaining to Kriesel. I continued to try and search him until he started drooling on me.

"Fuck this," I said to a laughing Kriesel. "He doesn't have any weapons on him. Even if he did, he couldn't use them anyway. I'm done." I dropped him back into his spot by the tree and left him to his drooling.

This was the man that Alpha Company saw as a big enough threat upon which to open fire. He was hit in the arm and brought to camp for medical treatment. He survived, but the villagers weren't very nice to us after that.

We spent the next couple of weeks moving from house to house and village to village taking a census of every household, compiling data on every adult

We looked really dirty and grizzled after our missions.

male in the house, their job, noting whether or not they had an AK-47. If they did, we wrote down the serial number.

After over two weeks away from Camp Fallujah without a shower, decent food, or a bed to sleep in, we finally finished our mission. Colonel Bristol was out there on the ground with us the entire time, doing the same things that the lowest private in the company was doing. I'm not sure whether or not we served up the big, cold bowl of fuck he had in mind, but we gave it our best shot.

CHAPTER 21:
Jimmy's Asian Brother

W HAT'S GOING ON, MY ASIAN BROTHER?" Jimmy asked Moua, who was wandering around in search of a roll of butt wipe. "What can I do for you?"

"I'm just looking for some TP so I can take a shit."

Seven months after our deployment ended, Specialist Luc Moua and I recalled the last day of Jimmy Wosika's life in a tearful conversation at a Chili's restaurant in Roseville, Minnesota. Jimmy had been Moua's team leader and the two had become close friends. "I don't know if that's something you want to put into the book, but it really meant a lot to me when he called me his 'Asian brother,'" Moua said, wiping the tears from his eyes.

The conversation Moua referred to took place in a house that 1st Squad took over to use as an OP. They had replaced my squad only a few hours earlier and were getting ready to patrol Zanti.

At 1500, 1st Squad left on patrol with Jimmy leading the way on the right side of the road and Moua and naval Corpsman Daniel "Doc" Fox following him. Goldstein led the way on the left side of the road with Dave the 'terp and Specialist David Stienbruckner behind him.

We shortened "Stienbruckner" to "Buckner" so it didn't take so damned long to talk to him. Buckner was a likable guy but always seemed to be in some kind of trouble with his superiors.

The patrol went smoothly at first. The guys stopped to ask a few men in the village some questions about their quality of living and what we could do to improve it. After two stops they noticed a small white pickup on the side

Doc Fox poses for a picture a few days before Jimmy's death.

of the road facing them. The truck had its hood open. Stalled cars and trucks were not unusual in Iraq because most people drove vehicles that were about twenty years old and had been poorly maintained.

Goldstein and Jimmy looked the stalled pickup over with their ACOG rifle scopes and decided that there wasn't anything fishy about it. Jimmy walked up to the truck and looked under the hood, while Goldstein approached on the left side.

When Jimmy finished checking things out under the hood, he walked around to the driver's side and looked in the window. That's when the truck blew up.

"When the truck exploded I saw Jimmy fly through the air," Moua recalled at lunch in Chili's. "After that I closed my eyes for a few seconds. I didn't think it was real until I opened my eyes and saw that both Jimmy and the truck were gone. I still see the image of Jimmy flying through the air sometimes." I had only heard bits and pieces of what happened to Jimmy. It's hard for us to talk about the details. It's hard to listen to the details, but that day at Chili's Moua told me the whole story:

"What just happened?" Doc yelled from the ground.

"That truck just exploded," I yelled back. "Where's Goldstein? Goldstein! Are you all right?"

Goldstein sat up and waved to let us know that he was okay, and then we shifted our focus to Jimmy.

"We gotta go find Jimmy," Doc told me. He and I walked along the row of cattails that ran along the little canal that the truck had been parked next to. We walked to where I thought I saw Jimmy land.

"What is that?" Doc asked me.

"That's his body armor." It was torn to shreds and hardly recognizable.

We walked a little further and I found Jimmy. I recognized the tattoos on his back. "Hey Doc, here he is."

"Okay, Moua. I don't think you should see this. I need you to pull security for me while I take care of Jimmy. Can you do that? I need you to do this for me."

"Okay. You're right."

A few minutes later, Goldstein showed up with Dave and Buckner. Buckner helped me provide security while Dave sat down out of the way.

"We found Jimmy," Doc told Goldstein. "You don't want to see him."

"Yeah, I do want to fucking see him," Goldstein said walking past Doc to see his friend. "Jimmy! Jimmy! Why Jimmy? Oh, Jimmy!"

Meanwhile, Moua explained, Sergeant Cannon Yang and Specialist Lee Vue drove up to the scene in two humvees. Yang, Vue, and Moua made up the "Asian Mafia." They were all Hmong and were a tight group of friends who always spoke Hmonglish, a pidgin mixture of English and Hmong that none of us could understand, making it difficult for us to join their conversations.

Moua and Slater before a raid.

"Moua, get into the gun on the humvee and pull security," Goldstein ordered Moua.

"What the fuck happened?" Cannon asked when Moua got into the humvee that Cannon was driving.

"Jimmy is gone," Moua said, after some hesitation.

Doc and Goldstein started to put Jimmy into a body bag while Moua, Cannon, and Dave went back to pack up their gear to move back to camp. The three marines who were assigned to 1st Squad were still in the house.

The three marines, Cannon, and Moua were packing up to leave when Moua saw that Dave was having trouble dealing with things.

"Dave, you have to get yourself together," Moua told him, trying to snap him out of his hysteria. "We need to get this shit packed up so we can get out of here."

Eventually, Dave stopped crying and pulled himself together long enough to get his shit packed. A little while later, QRF and EOD showed up to take control of the scene and bring Jimmy's body back to base. Once QRF had everything under control, 1st Squad drove back to base.

When they got back they met the rest of us in the motor pool, where the platoon helped them out of their trucks and gear before we went to say goodbye to Jimmy.

"I'd always wanted to get to know Jimmy a little better," I said to Moua at the end of our conversation in Chili's. "I just never got around to it. I really feel bad about that."

"Yeah, Jimmy was a great guy," Moua told me. "He just really fucking loved junk food." To someone else it might have seemed an odd detail to remember about a dead friend, but having been through the same thing myself—having nothing left of Corey but a bunch of random memories—I understood what he meant completely.

CHAPTER 22:
The Devil's Children

THROUGHOUT THE CHAOS SURROUNDING JIMMY'S DEATH, I felt nothing. I was fucking numb. It was like I had spent all the emotional currency I had when Dunna and Corey died and now I was bankrupt.

No one from home had said anything to me after Dunna and Corey died, but for some reason almost everyone I knew emailed me after Jimmy died, and they all said the same thing: "Hey Nick, I heard about the accident. I'm sorry for your loss." It infuriated me. It wasn't a fucking accident. There was nothing accidental about what happened to Jimmy or Corey or Dunna. The miserable pieces of shit who killed them did it on purpose. I wrote scathing email responses to each and every one of them, but I didn't send any of them. I might have sent them eventually, but sand got in my hard drive and my computer took a shit.

I knew I could be next. Any illusions I'd had about being invulnerable died with Corey and Dunna. But I didn't fucking care if I lived or died. I went out wondering which pile of debris covered the explosives that were going to blow me up, but I didn't fucking care.

About five days after Jimmy died we had a memorial service for him. I went to the chapel the morning of the service and hung out for a while with Colonel Bristol and some other guys. Bristol made fun of my haircut: "Specialist Maurstad, what the fuck is wrong with your hair? Did they just put a bowl on your head and cut around it." I considered saying, "Yes sir, a big cold bowl of fuck," but since Bristol was a personal friend of Chuck Norris, I couldn't discount the possibility that he would kill me by smashing my septum

When the neighbors brought us chai the interpreter would have the first cup to ensure it wasn't poisoned. Martin liked to pretend that it was.

into my brain with the heel of his hand. So I just laughed and blamed it on our Turkish barbers.

Bristol joked with us, but he was seriously upset by Jimmy's death.

We went into the chapel, took our seats, and the memorial started. The Elicerio wasn't there this time—he must have taken Colonel Bristol's warning to heart. The service was pretty much the same as the one for Dunna and Corey. Bristol was the first person to speak. "I'm a professional marine," he told us. "This is what I dedicated my life to. Jimmy and I used to wrestle. Because I was the professional, I couldn't let Jimmy win. Jimmy was a talented wrestler and driven to win, but because I was a professional, I made sure I beat him." Bristol, this bull of a man, stood up in front of us choking back his tears so he could keep speaking. "If I had to do it over again, I'd let him win every time.

"I had to go identify Jimmy's body. That's part of being a professional. The

210

Enjoying chai complete with British tea faces.

only way I could identify the body was because of his tattoos, which I'd seen when we were wrestling.

"I'll continue to go on being a professional. I'll continue to do this job. But I wish that Jimmy, and people like Jimmy who aren't professional soldiers, could just go home and live in peace."

The other commanders spoke and then some of Jimmy's friends spoke. The whole time I sat in the middle of the crowd, emotionless. I was completely numb.

Then the service was over and we went back to our jobs. And our jobs were never the same after that. We'd ratcheted up our aggression after Dunna and Corey died. After Jimmy died, we became downright ruthless. A lot of the other guys seemed to feel like me, numb and not really giving a fuck about anything. Or else they felt angry, filled with rage and hatred toward the Iraqis. We didn't care if we lived or died, and we didn't much care if the Iraqis did

We liked to play pranks on the Iraqis.

either. It got ugly and it got brutal. Before, the Iraqis had been standoffish but courteous—they didn't fuck with us and we didn't fuck with them. Sometimes they even brought us bread and chai tea. After Jimmy died, we turned into monsters and they would hide in their houses whenever they saw us.

Later one of our 'terps told me that after we'd turned into ruthless, brutal bastards, the locals had started calling soldiers wearing the Red Bull insignia on their uniforms "the devil's children."

CHAPTER 23:
The Elicerio

O UR EXTENSION IN IRAQ CAME DOWN ON US like a million-pound shit hammer. Instead of beginning a week in Fort McCoy, Wisconsin, decompressing from a year spent fighting in Anbar Province and preparing to return home in March, 2007, we were crammed into an airless room in Fallujah, breathing the almost palpable stench of our own sweating balls.

At two in the morning I couldn't sleep. I needed to rest up for another day of foot patrols; instead I lay in my cot, reeling under a blur of semi-conscious images from the past: a fast-forward stream of faces and blown-up humvees and Iraqis cowering naked behind kicked-down doors. I tried to ignore the images, but finally gave in and let my imagination play out.

The lead character in my brain movie, a colonel who called himself the Elicerio, the miserable cocksucker in charge of the Minnesota National Guard, sat in a conference room with the other brigade commanders in Iraq. I imagined the Elicerio not dressed in appropriate military attire, but in a pink leotard with a fluffy tutu and a little princess tiara perched atop his towering watery forehead. While all of the other commanders around the table shuffled notebooks and papers, preparing for the big meeting to decide who would stay in Iraq for the surge, the Elicerio arranged his prized collection of My Little Pony action figurines in an elaborate diorama.

In my half-awake imagination, no one in the room seemed to find this out of the ordinary. When General Casey entered, everyone stood at attention except the Elicerio, who only glanced up with his lazy eye; his dominant eye remained fixed on his My Little Pony figurines, which were

The Elicerio shares a traditional Iraqi meal with his security staff and a half dozen cabbage patch dolls. *Minnesota National Guard*

engaged in a reenactment of the Battle of Bannockburn. (Rumor had it that the Elicerio was inspired to incorporate the article into his name by his hero, Robert the Bruce.)

The general got right down to business. "Good morning, gentlemen. I hope we can wrap this up by lunch time. If this surge that the president is pushing for is going to happen, we'll have to extend one of the brigades for four months. We will not leave this room until we decide which brigade it will be, so I'll start by asking for a volunteer."

The general's words momentarily ripped through the Elicerio's bone-heavy skull and spurred the formulation of something vaguely resembling abstract thought. His lazy eye uncrossed and some of the slack went out of his drool-covered jaw. His chronically short attention shifted away from his My-Little-Bannockburn fantasy and he exerted an almost superhuman effort to concentrate on what the general was saying. *Volunteer?* he thought. *I don't know what the general wants us to volunteer for, but maybe if I volunteer, the*

other commanders won't tease me so much about my beautiful little ponies.
Maybe they'll give me one of those cool stars to wear on my leotard. The Elicerio
leapt from his chair and flapped his arms like the vestigial wings of a flightless
bird whose reptilian brain stem had glommed on to some ancestral flight
instinct. "Pick me! Pick me!" he screamed like a six-year-old trying to get the
attention of a circus clown so he could be the first to ride the elephant.

"Well, I guess that settles that," the general said as he got up from his chair.
"Lunch is on me." The serene smile I imagined crossing the Elicerio's face as
he returned to his imaginary Battle of Bannockburn, urging his My Cowardly
Little Earl of Gloucester against a brigade of My Little Scots Spearmen, calmed
me and I fell into a deep, dreamless sleep.

CHAPTER 24:
Three Swords

T HE DAY BEFORE OUR NEXT BIG MISSION, Operation Three Swords, Nelly briefed our squad about what we would be doing. We looked over pictures of Haythem Kudar Muhammad, an ex-Iraqi intelligence officer suspected of running a torture house who was to be our target for the mission. Nelly gave us a description of his physical appearance (fat cocksucker), brief life story (brutal cocksucker), and aerial photos of his house (rich cocksucker). He kind of looked like Hassel, only fatter, which was pretty fat since we called Hassel "Butter Ball." I nicknamed Haythem "Fat Hassel." We made a plan for going in and were told to be ready for anything.

That evening we spent rehearsing. We set up a mock house with two-by-fours laid on the ground to map out rooms and doors. Once Nelly was comfortable that everyone knew their jobs during the raid, we went back to our rooms to finish preparing our gear for the mission. For the first time I was nervous about the mission. I walked to the phone center to call my family.

"I am going on a mission tomorrow night, and I really have a bad feeling about it," I told my dad when I got him on the phone.

"What are you going to be doing?" he asked.

"I can't tell you anything about it, but I really just don't feel good about it. I don't have a lot of time to talk tonight. I just wanted to tell you I love you before I left. I'll call you when I get back."

"I love you too, kid." We said goodbye and I made a few more similar calls before I went to my room to sleep.

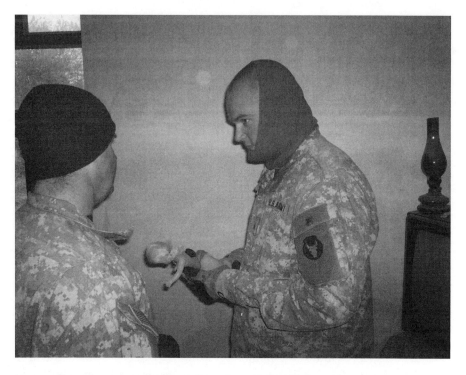

Horn prepares to use a Barbie doll to show Jones his legendary sexual technique.

The next night we gathered in the motor pool to get ready to go. When our trucks were set up and our gear was in order, we stood around drinking an energy drink similar to Red Bull called Wild Tiger, but we called it "Tiger Piss." Drinks in hand, we joked about who was going to get killed in Zydon during our mission that night. It was the only way to deal with our nervousness.

Just before we left, I taped a Mini Maglite to end of the barrel of the shotgun I would be carrying that night. I jumped into the truck and we took off.

We drove to the south gate of camp and loaded our weapons before we left. The large column of humvees and Bradleys left the gate at 2200. We drove almost two hundred meters outside the gate before we stopped.

Lieutenant Casey, the company executive officer and convoy commander, was already lost, which was about the level of leadership we expected from the

218

Chris Ness Flies the Jolly Roger from a humvee antennae.

fucktard. Casey drove about one hundred meters past the turn to the overpass across the major highway that ran near the camp. He spent the next twenty minutes trying to figure out the location of the ramp to the overpass, even though we could all see it sitting in the middle of a stretch of barren desert.

Once Lieutenant Casey the rocket scientist unfucked himself, we started moving again. A few miles down the road the Meerkat (the new EOD vehicle that had just then gone into service) hit an IED. The vehicle itself is nearly indestructible, and when it hits an IED, the explosion just blows the wheels off. No one in the Meerkat is usually hurt by an IED, but the drivers tend to be on the nervous side and always look like they hate life. A truck carrying extra sets of wheels follows the Meerkat and when the Meerkat hits a bomb, the crew simply mounts another set of wheels on the vehicle. Ninety minutes after

Yogi got creative drawing a variation of the pissing boy picture on the back of this humvee turret.

the Meerkat in our mission hit the IED, the crew had replaced the wheels and we began to move again.

We finally arrived at our target house at 0100. Buda helped me get the radio into the pouch I had on my back. We left the trucks with the gunners on the road while we ran up to the house.

I stood beside the door and waited for Micheletti to kick it in, like we had rehearsed the night before. The door flew open behind his size nine. I turned on the Mini Maglite I had taped to the barrel of my shotgun and rushed into the room. I covered my section of the room. The rest of the squad followed so close behind me that someone stepped on my heels.

We cleared the large, empty core room of the house in seconds. Buda watched the door through which we had just entered the house, and the rest of

220

Me sitting in an Iraqi house trying to choke down an MRE.

Kohler cleans his weapon.

us lined up in front of the four wooden doors leading to different rooms. Two men apiece lined up in front of three of the doors, and I was the odd man out standing alone in front of my door. Nelly counted to three and we all kicked our doors down and went in. I stormed the room, my shotgun shouldered and my heart pounding. My small flashlight provided the only light in the room. I made a quick appraisal of the inhabitants in the dim light and made out five freshly woken and terrified toddlers on the floor. When I looked left I saw the mother sitting up next to her husband. I moved toward the male who was only halfway upright, with his right hand digging under his pillow. He produced a pistol and, with three quick steps, my muzzle was within inches of his face. I stomped on his hand and kicked the gun away before he could point it at me. To this day I don't understand why I didn't just wax the fat bastard, but somehow I managed to refrain from pulling the shotgun trigger and spraying his brains all over his terrified family.

I yelled at him to keep his hands up and not move, but I was yelling in a language he didn't understand. My shouting caught Nelly's attention and he rushed in to assist me.

"What do you have in here, Maurstad?" He asked when he entered the room.

"He tried to shoot me," I explained with my shotgun still trained on the guy's face.

"This is our guy!" Nelly shouted as he reached down to drag the overweight man out of the room. I'd caught Fat Hassel. "We got him! Woo hoo!"

When Nelly started dragging Fat Hassel out of the room, the man's wife started yelling and holding her husband back. I remedied the problem by yelling louder than her and putting a 12-gauge shotgun in her face.

I noticed that the sweater Fat Hassel was wearing only covered about half of his fat belly as the blankets started to slide off of him. When Nelly pulled him further from the bed, his pantless lower half was uncovered, revealing Fat Hassel's junk, which was quickly ascending up into the scared motherfucker's massive cavity. Judging from the position in which I'd found Fat Hassel and his wife, I'd kicked in the door while the fat bastard's wife was sucking his cock, which is probably the only reason he wasn't ready to shoot when I came busting through the door. My life had been saved by a blowjob.

Fat Hassel's wife grabbed his pants and handed them to me. When I adjusted my grip on the weapon to take his pants, I realized that my finger was still on the trigger and the safety was off. I flicked the switch back to safe and handed the pants to Nelly, who was making fun of Fat Hassel's shriveled penis while he dragged him out of the room.

I rounded up Fat Hassel's wife and children and gave them to Horn, who was gathering all of the women and children into a room out of our way. When the room was empty, I began searching it.

The first thing I found was an AK-47 fully loaded with three magazines taped together for quick reloading. It was in plain sight, leaning against the dresser two feet from the bed. If Fat Hassel had been holding that instead of his junk when I'd busted through the door, I probably wouldn't be here writing this down. I unloaded the rifle and threw it onto the fast growing pile of weapons in the main room. I continued to tear apart the room and found two more AKs and a few big wads of cash.

When I finished searching the room, I moved into the main room where Doc watched the men of the house who were all lying face down on the floor. The shitty washing machine in the corner caught my eye. I walked across the room to check it out.

I tore the lid off without much resistance and found it full of unwashed clothes. Thinking it would be a perfect place to hide some more weapons, I dug the contents out.

A hand grenade fell out of the second handful of clothes I pulled out of the machine. It was the World War II pineapple-style grenade that Sergeant First Class Hawkins had told us to worry about during our training at Camp Shelby.

When I saw it land I closed my eyes as tight as I could and stood there like an idiot after I yelled "Grenade!" to the rest of the squad. I bit my lower lip for the longest ten seconds of my life before I accepted the fact that I wasn't going to be blown to shreds. Surprised to be alive, I carefully picked up the grenade and found the pin still in place. I set it down in a safe spot and kept digging.

Near the bottom, I discovered an ammo vest with a few more magazines in it and two black ski masks. The evidence that this was a very bad man was piling up fast. With the deaths of my three close friends still fresh in my mind, I started to regret my decision to not shoot Fat Hassel when I had the chance. To this day I regret not pulling the trigger and turning his head into a fine red paste.

Nelly took the handset on the radio that was attached to my back and tried to call in a progress report. We were not getting reception, so we went up to the roof for better reception. We called the Bradleys to come and transport our detainees to the holding area. Then we were given another target to compensate for another squad that was bogged down in a different house. We were supposed to capture three brothers at this house. No one told us why we were supposed to catch them, but the question "why" is not one that comes up much in combat missions.

Once the detainees were hauled away, we got back into our trucks. I kept the radio on my back to speed things up. I drove to the next house with the

Nelly and Micheletti spar before a mission.

radio pushing me forward, hunching me over my steering wheel like a ninety-six-year-old man.

We parked next to the second target house and stacked up by the front door. I was given the first crack at kicking the door down. I stepped in front of it and put all 270 pounds of myself and my gear into the door via my foot. My knee went backwards and I fell on my ass. The door appeared to be rock solid until Micheletti gave it a shot. An expert at door kicking, Micheletti dropped the door and we stormed in, waking the inhabitants.

We found the entire family in one room of the house. We pulled them out of that room and into the center room. Four out of the five family members moved without any struggle. The oldest son, about thirteen, refused to stand up or let go of his blankets. Once he was forcibly separated from the blanket, we saw that he was sporting a woody and was extremely embarrassed about it. We dragged him into the room with the others, laughing at his boner while he cried and tried to hide it from his family. I had to admire a guy who could

Nelly gives the squad the mission briefing before Operation Three Swords.

remain rock hard while a bunch of foreign soldiers with guns dragged him out of bed in the middle of the night. The kid could have a career in porn if he wanted.

We took the men with us to the newly added target house so we could send them to the company firm base for questioning later in the morning. On the walk there, the father pretended to have a heart attack and collapsed in an attempt to gain some sympathy and be released. He didn't understand that we weren't taking him away for good.

When we arrived at our new target, we found three houses in a small group. Not sure which house we were supposed to raid, we went through them

226

one at a time. The first two houses didn't have anyone in them so we searched them and moved on.

In the third house, we found the three brothers we were supposed to capture. We found the first two asleep in their rooms. They cooperated and came into the center room with no problems. While Nelly and Horn questioned them with the 'terp, the rest of us searched the house. I searched one small room and moved on to help Doc Dinsmore search the next one.

"How's it going in here?" I asked when I walked into the room.

"Fine," he replied. "I'm about done in here. I haven't found anything." I searched a bit more aggressively than Doc. I pulled a large pile of blankets and floor mats apart and tried to kick around a pile on the floor in the corner. It didn't move as I expected it to.

"What the fuck is this?" I asked Dinsmore when I pulled one of the blankets off of the pile, revealing the third brother who pretended that I couldn't see him.

"Holy shit!" Doc shouted. "How did I miss him?" Still reluctant to accept that he had been found, the heavy-set man hunkered down into an even tighter fetal position, as if that would make him invisible. I kicked him in the back progressively harder until he finally stood up. Once on his feet, he tried to pretend that he was deathly sick. Not being fooled by his extremely bad acting, I dragged his ass into the other room with his brothers.

"This dipshit was hiding in a pile of blankets," I told Nelly, dragging the man by the collar of his shirt. "Now he's trying to play sick."

"All right, contestant number three, come on down!" Nelly said, happy to have the third brother in custody.

We took our five detainees a couple houses down, to where Sergeant Adam Gallant, Kohler, Chris Ness, and Yogi waited for us.

A Bradley picked up our detainees and we took a three-hour break. I sat down in a corner without taking off my gear and passed out from exhaustion. An hour later Horn woke me up and sent me up to the roof to guard the house while others slept. I sat up there for two hours watching the unspectacular Iraqi sunrise before I was relieved.

Just as I sat down to go to sleep, we were called to watch a road. We left a few guys and a humvee at the house, while Micheletti, Nelly, Horn, and I sat in the cab of another humvee and Grub stood in the gun turret. We were supposed to watch the road for locals moving around, but I fell into semi-consciousness in the backseat of the humvee, maintaining just enough awareness to hear the radio chatter calling for an air medevac for an Iraqi. Later I found out that he'd been rescued from an insurgent torture house found by 3rd Platoon, one of three Iraqi army soldiers who were saved. One was found barely alive, chained to a bed with both of his arms and legs broken. He'd been burned and both of his kneecaps had been shattered. He must have had a pretty tough time of it, judging by the syringes, clubs, knives, and blowtorches they found in the torture house.

An hour later we were still sitting on the road, all nodding off. We tried to make conversation to stay awake, but it was mostly the incoherent babble that comes out of a person's mouth when he is somewhere between awake and asleep.

"Holy fuck!" Micheletti yelled, shocking us all awake.

We looked out the window in the direction he pointed and saw a huge mushroom cloud coming up behind some trees. The sound hit us a second later.

"Net call, net call. There will be a controlled det. in one minute," the radio explained, warning everyone in the area of the explosion that had just happened ten seconds earlier.

Colonel Bristol decided to make an example of the torture house we found. He did this by lining it with a couple hundred pounds of C-4 and blowing it to smithereens.

Shortly after the house exploded, we were sent to help 3rd Platoon with their area. We spent the rest of the morning and afternoon running from house to house, tearing everything apart looking for weapons.

When we finished the raid around 1500, we were all completely exhausted. We were sitting in a ditch when our lieutenant started to get ideas. He ordered a Bradley to blow up a boat on the riverbank to keep people from escaping.

Buda and I had run some papers to the lieutenant in a house a few hundred yards away, and I heard the call on the radio while we were on our way back to our squad. I told Buda about it and he asked if he could film it since he had never seen a Bradley fire its 25mm gun before, so we stopped while the Bradley fired seven shots at the boat.

A Bradley drives through Zydon.

When the Bradley was finished we rejoined our squad. We found everyone sitting in a ditch while our platoon sergeant, Sergeant First Class Myrold, flipped out.

He had not heard the call warning everyone about the Bradley firing. Thinking there was a gunfight nearby he reacted like the douchebag he was—he pulled a guy out of the humvee, jumped in, closed the door for safety, and cowered inside the cab. Once he realized that the shots were coming from one of our Bradleys, he decided to play the hero and get everyone to go attack whatever it was that the Bradley was shooting at. He hadn't been listening to his radio, so he didn't know that the lieutenant had just sunk an empty boat. When I got there, Myrold was running around like a spastic meth addict, trying to get everyone to go all commando and attack something, anything. When I explained what had happened, he pretended he knew all along and that he hadn't been acting like a cowardly twat. Once Myrold calmed down we moved everyone to the house we'd been at earlier in the morning and waited to leave.

Near the end of the convoy, we sat on the side of the road waiting for the rest of the column to pass. When our spot came, we got in line just in time for the front of the convoy to hit an IED and stop. It was 1730 and the sun was going down.

The convoy continued an hour later and hit another IED just a few kilometers down the road. The ride back to camp took eight hours while the lead vehicles hit IED after IED.

When we finally got back to camp we parked the humvees and put the machine guns away. Everyone was sent to bed except for Horn and me. The detainees we took back to camp had to have their paperwork processed. Horn always did the paperwork because he was good at it. Gallant normally helped him but because he was a fucking prick, he told me to do it while he went to bed.

For the next four hours Horn and I wrote statements, evidence lists, and filled out forms with the detainees' identification information and our contact information. We also questioned one of the brothers about the torture house. He gave up a bunch of information about the other brothers involved in the torture cell, hoping that we would give him special treatment. We didn't.

I finally got to sleep at 0600. I slept for eighteen hours, only getting up to piss once. It was the best sleep I had gotten in over a year.

CHAPTER 25:
Flanders' Hunting Safari

I GOT THE LITTLE BASTARD!" Winnie shouted after bagging his third coyote. "Let's go have a look at him." Winnie, Seed, and Chris Ness walked over to look at the dead coyote. I'd seen enough dead coyotes and stayed back in the tower we'd been using as a hunting stand. Besides, I was on duty and supposed to stay back. Not that being on duty mattered much anymore—it was February, 2007, and we were about a month away from starting our extension; by that time we were doubling up on our daily dose of Fuck-It-All.

We were on our final stay at Pump House Flanders before we turned it over to the marines. We didn't know for sure that we weren't coming back, but we suspected that we were going to be done at Flanders after the extensions started. We thought we might be going to work with the battalion in TQ, which was the least likely option, according to what Captain Rankin told us. If we stayed in Camp Fallujah we figured we would be going out on more raids like Three Swords and Sledgehammer, which we thought was the most-likely scenario. We'd had so much success doing these sorts of operations that we figured they'd keep us doing that. Either way, we most likely wouldn't come back to Flanders.

On that final stay, we developed a more offensive method of guarding the place. Instead of just sitting next to a machine gun waiting to return fire in the event of an attack, we started firing our rifles as often as possible, shooting

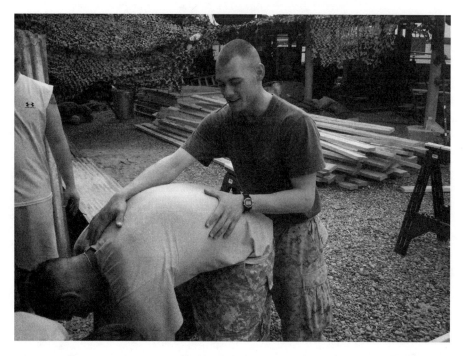

Miller shows Nelly why you never bend over in the desert around a bunch of horny soldiers. Immediately after this photo was taken, Nelly showed Miller why you don't try to sodomize someone who is bigger and stronger than you.

everything we could shoot without getting in trouble. That meant we could basically shoot everything that moved except Iraqis and each other.

We used every bit of the technology that the military provided for us to find things to shoot. One item that proved particularly useful was the FLIR camera. This was an infrared video camera mounted on a twenty-five-foot mast inside the compound. An operator in a small building below the mast could rotate the camera 360 degrees, scanning the perimeter. I designed and built the building from substandard, mismatched lumber. My dad is a carpenter and had taught me a lot when I was a kid, so it turned out pretty solid anyway. At least the floor was level, unlike the barracks building 3rd Squad built.

The person running the FLIR camera scanned the perimeter of the compound out to about two hundred meters. Whenever he found a hot spot moving around, he radioed the position to a small team waiting in our shitty

We became bored enough to start branding ourselves. Corporal Chris Ness has branded himself with the letter "N," presumably for "Ness."

excuse of a lounge. This team consisted of at least two shooters and a shiner. When the camera operator called the team and told them that something was moving outside the perimeter, the team went out to the area where the camera operator spotted the movement. Once the team was in place peering over the wall, they would locate the hot spot with a portable FLIR and night-vision goggles.

With the spot located and everyone ready to fire, the shiner illuminated the spot with the 15 million candle-power spotlight, which we normally used to check out suspicious things at night—and also to wake each other up. Once the heat source was confirmed as an animal of some kind and not some confused Iraqi, the shooters opened up on it and blasted it to shreds. After a while we figured out that if we used MREs as bait, we could get a lot more hunting action going.

This went on for nearly a week, taking a serious toll on our supply of shitty food. We used the most nauseating MREs—the cheese omelet MRE,

Corporal Chris Ness holds Cringer, the kitten we kept at Pump House Flanders.

the jambalaya MRE, and cheese-coated chicken tortellini MRE—for bait. The coyotes couldn't resist this noxious slop, but then they also lick their own assholes.

We took out our frustration at being extended because of the surge, and our rage at losing our friends, out on all the cuddly, furry little creatures that came within two hundred meters of Flanders: coyotes, rabbits, marmots, stray cats. We didn't get any dogs because after Blomgren instituted his dog genocide policy, the Iraqis kept the surviving dogs close to home.

I enjoyed this Flanders safari and didn't mind shooting anything except for the cats. It wasn't because I had never killed a cat before. I grew up on a farm with lots of cats living in the sheds and barns. We fed these cats, but they were semi-feral and none of them were spayed or neutered. Every once in a while the cats would have so many kittens that they would become an infestation. The traditional method for dealing with an infestation of anything on a farm is mass extermination, and we were nothing if not traditional.

It never bothered me when we had to clean the farm of cats, but I felt bad about killing these particular cats at Flanders because they were likely related to the little kitten we had been keeping as a pet a few months earlier.

Nelly found the kitten, which we named "Cringer," after the cat in *He-Man and the Masters of the Universe*, while he was out on a patrol one day. Its cuteness proved irresistible and he brought it back to Flanders. The cat was a huge morale booster and the entire platoon loved the little thing. The cat seemed extremely happy with the arrangement too, probably because we gave it a regular food supply.

We gave the cat a comfortable life over its next few weeks at Flanders. Kriesel built a little cat house for it, we fed it MREs and tuna from the PX, and someone was holding it or playing with it all day long.

Corporal Chris Ness enjoys a cigar and a beautiful Iraqi sunrise.

Eventually, Sergeant Major O'Connell came to the pump house with Bristol and found the cat being kept as a pet. He told us that we couldn't keep the cat for health reasons. Figuring the most humane way to deal with the cat was to kill it instead of letting it starve outside the walls, O'Connell decided to euthanize it.

Specialist Ness couldn't bear to see the little guy harmed, so he threw the cat across the canal like a hand grenade. It landed on its feet and didn't seem hurt, but it was upset over the mistreatment and ran away. The cat missed its food supply, so it came back the next day. It sat on the other side of the canal for a day and a half, waiting for us to rescue it, but the nearest canal crossing was over a mile away so we couldn't do anything about it.

On the second day it decided to brave the raging waters of the canal and swim home. Its tiny little body was no match for the current and it was swept away, never to be seen again. Ness felt terrible about it, and he got especially upset when we teased him about being a heartless kitten murderer.

CHAPTER 26:
"Dan, You're a Pussy"

In late February 2007 a group of high ranking military commanders visited Camp Fallujah. During the commanders' visit, we were sent to raid a group of small villages on the eastern edge of our AO. Being out there made us decoys to distract the insurgents from firing mortars at camp.

Lieutenant Blomgren led the platoon from Pump House Flanders at 0100. The platoon marched at speeds exceeding Mach 2 for about three miles. Despite the forty-degree February weather, I was sweating through my shirt. With a mile to go, Blomgren realized that we would arrive nearly two hours early. The mission couldn't begin until the VIP's helicopter landed, so we stopped in a palm grove and waited.

We sat there for an hour and a half, nearly freezing to death when the low temperature cooled our sweat-soaked shirts. Just when I was sure hypothermia was setting in, Blomgren gave the order to move out. We got back into our marching order and resumed our grueling pace into the first village.

My squad got to the first house and tried to open the door. When it didn't open right away, Horn turned around and told us we needed to breach it. Horn and I unstrapped the door breaching tools that Buda had on his back. I turned around with a maul, while Horn fought with the straps holding the pry bar in place.

When I turned around, I saw that Grub had interpreted Horn's words differently. He was positioned to shoot the lock out of the door with his shotgun and pulled the trigger a split second after I turned to witness it.

Up to this point, shooting the lock off of a stubborn door had been an easy and acceptable way to get into a building. The issue this time was that the commander wanted to keep the element of surprise for as long as possible.

"What the fuck was that!" Nelly yelled, pissed off that the element of surprise had been blown in the first five minutes of the mission by a shotgun blast.

"We couldn't get the door open, so I said that we needed to breach it and then Grub just shot it when I was turned around trying to get this crowbar," Horn piped up in classic Horn fashion.

"Nice fucking work, guys. You just fucked the entire mission over. Well, nothing we can do now. Let's get into this building."

We turned our attention back to the door, which now featured a shotgun hole. Despite having its lock shot out we still couldn't get the door open. Horn jammed the pry bar in between the door and the jam and pried, while I pounded on it with the maul. This charade continued for nearly five minutes before we gave up.

Just when all seemed lost, the door practically swung open by itself. When the door was fully open, we saw a decrepit old woman who looked as if she would fall over and die if she was exposed to even the slightest of breezes.

We began our search of the house and found the entire family curled up under one pile of blankets trying to beat the cold. When we tried to get the father out of bed to talk to him, he started shrieking like a six-year-old girl while his wife and six-year-old girl sat calmly watching.

Eventually the man calmed down enough so we could talk to him. We asked him if he had a job, how safe his village was, and if his daughter was in school. Before we left we took the bolt out of his AK-47 and threw it into his yard as a safety precaution.

We went into another house, which was a typical Iraqi house with a central room and doors leading off that room to the other rooms in the house. We each took a door and kicked it in. There was nothing behind my door, which was across the room from Horn's door. I heard him yell, "Holy shit!" and turned around to see a naked woman standing behind his kicked-down door. She wasn't just any naked woman, either. She was smoking hot by any standard, American or Iraqi. Her long black hair hung past her face, which looked pretty even though she was screaming her lungs out. Her breasts were large, but not

The side of the road washed out into the canal and overturned the Bradley. Water flooded the driver's compartment and turret.

out of proportion to her body—standard C cups. They rode high on her chest, as one would expect from a woman in her mid-twenties, their big, brown nipples poking out like pencil erasers because of the cold. Her bushy pube-fest was a bit shocking to my eyes, which were used to seeing the neatly trimmed landing strips most American women had covering their vaginas, but her legs and hips were so shapely that the big, furry beaver didn't phase me.

We let her get dressed before moving her to another room. Every time we went into a house, we put all the adult males in one room and the women and children in a separate room. While Horn and Nelly questioned the men, I glanced into the room where the women were and saw one of these fine tits once again exposed; the woman was breast-feeding her infant. I tried not to be obvious about staring at her boob as I watched her feed her baby.

30/01/2007

The mechanics pulled the Bradley out of the water and upright with an M-88. The water and mud damaged the Bradley beyond repair.

The rest of the mission went smoothly. The squads leapfrogged each other, running from house to house. At the end of the last village, we occupied a house where most of the squad took a nap while we waited for the truck to pick us up and shuttle us back to Flanders.

After we'd waited about an hour, one of the Bradleys rolled into the canal. It was just before dawn when the side of the road collapsed into the water, pulling the Bradley in with it. The Bradley rolled over on its top, trapping Hoiland and Wallace in the turret.

Ness crawled to the troop compartment to help rescue Hoiland and Wallace. Outside the crew from the rear Bradley jumped into the canal, still wearing their body armor, and tried to help their brothers escape.

In the turret Wallace was stuck upside down in his seat with his face in the water. Accepting that he would drown to death in his overturned Bradley, Wallace inhaled a mouthful of water. A second later Hoiland managed to free him and Wallace coughed up the water he had just inhaled. Ness pulled Wallace and Hoiland out of the turret and out of the Bradley through the small troop door in the back, which had been opened by the guys outside.

While the clusterfuck to recover the overturned Bradley developed, my platoon moved to the house that Colonel Bristol was in with his marine entourage, a few soldiers from our headquarters platoon. Bristol took this opportunity to chat with a few of us.

During the conversation, he brought up our old commander Captain Dan Murphy. "Your old commander was a really great garrison commander. He understood how to conduct training, was always wearing a clean and neat uniform, and was really proper and followed military customs and courtesies.

"But one day I just had enough, so I called him into my offices and I said to him, 'Dan, you're a pussy,' and I fired him."

Shortly after our chat was over, our truck came and brought us back to Camp Fallujah.

Captain Chip Rankin stands at the front of the company formation. *Minnesota National Guard*

CHAPTER 27:
Goodbye Camp Fallujah

About a week after Ness rescued Wallace and Hoiland from the Bradley, Colonel Bristol and Sergeant Major O'Connell left Camp Fallujah. Their tours were up and when they left, they took with them all of the marines who had worked with us everyday. These men had become our brothers and, while we were happy they were getting to go home, we were going to miss them. The whole company gathered to hear Bristol and O'Connell bid us farewell.

"This is one of the finest organizations of men that I have ever had the privilege of working with," O'Connell said in his farewell speech. "I know that some of you probably wouldn't appreciate it, but I would like nothing more than to put every one of you in a marine uniform and take you with me.

"You remind me of another Bravo Company that I was a part of earlier in my career. They, like you, were hard working, very proficient at their jobs, and the men were extremely close. Like them, this Bravo Company will always have a special place in my heart. This will not be the last time we meet, I assure you that. The colonel and I will see you in Fort McCoy when you get back to the States. Until then I want all of you to keep doing your jobs and get home safe."

When O'Connell was through speaking, he stepped to the side so Colonel Bristol could give his speech: "Men, you've done a great job for me. I respect and appreciate everything you've done. I will be back here within the next year.

Colonel George H. Bristol delivers his farewell address to the company.
Minnesota National Guard

My only hope is that you men go back to the lakes and rivers of Minnesota and live in peace, and that you never have to return to this place again. I'll see all of you when you return home. I'll be in Fort McCoy waiting for you."

We'd sort of hoped for some crazy, homicidal Bristolism, but he kept it brief. We could tell he meant every word he said and we appreciated it. Every one of us felt honored to have had the opportunity to serve under these men. There wasn't one person in the company who didn't think that Bristol's becoming our commander was the best thing that had happened to us in Iraq. No one would ever have expected a little company of the Minnesota National Guard to serve under marine leadership of the caliber of Bristol and O'Connell. After they'd given their speeches, Bristol walked over and kissed our guidon, then both men went through our ranks and said goodbye to every single man in the company. They thanked us for our service, gave us a hug, and slapped us

Bristol got pretty excited and animated with his delivery. *Minnesota National Guard*

on our backs. The hug and slap on the back from Colonel Bristol knocked the wind right out of us. It was like saying goodbye to a grizzly bear.

After Bristol and the rest of the marines left, we began training the marines who would be replacing us. We took them out on a patrol to show them our AO and told them as much as we could about what was going on in the different villages. The marines seemed eager to learn all that they could, but we didn't have much time to teach them.

Their commander was no Bristol, and he didn't seem to have much respect for us. For the first time in months, we were being treated as "just a national guard company." The new marine commander either didn't believe the reputation we had earned or had just never bothered to learn anything about us. This made it hard to train the marines who were replacing us, because their commander seemed pissed off about the notion that a lowly national

I wait for my turn to say goodbye to Colonel Bristol. His hugs kind of hurt.
Minnesota National Guard

guard company could teach the marines anything. He seemed to think that on the off chance our experience could be of some use to his men, whatever pathetic information we might have could surely be transmitted in one day. The incoming commander's overdeveloped marine ego screwed his men out of a lot of important information when we handed the AO over to him.

While we were doing our best to educate the new marines in our last day of work in Fallujah, the company leadership was handing over all of the intelligence we had gathered over the last year, including the census we had done.

The marines replacing Bristol's men thought they would have to take a census of the villages southeast of the city. When they arrived they found that we'd already done the job for them. Instead of taking the work we did and using that information to change the focus of their mission, they deleted the

Bristol hugs Sergeant Halvorson, a soldier in third platoon, before he leaves.
Eric Bowen

computer files containing all of the census information so they could do it themselves. As we were packing to leave, they realized how stupid this had been and asked us if we had kept a copy. We hadn't.

Three days later, on March 5, 2007, we left Camp Fallujah to serve our four-month extension on Camp Taqaddum. I spent the day packing everything that was left in my room and cleaning the barracks building. That night, after everything was packed and clean, we moved to the helicopter pad to wait for a flight to our new home.

While we waited at the airstrip, Jones said, "Man, this is fucked up. We should be waiting for our fucking ride home right now."

"No shit," I replied. We spent the next few minutes quietly pondering the statement. We were still bitter about our extension. We described the situation with the acronym BOHICA—bend over, here it comes again.

After a couple hours of waiting, our bird finally showed up. We grabbed our gear and shuffled to the waiting CH-46. We took off a few minutes later. As we ascended, I watched the camp get smaller and I became a little bit sad. I felt the same as I did when I had left home a year and a half earlier.

When we got to Camp Taqaddum I moved into my room with Yogi. Our rooms consisted of small shipping containers manufactured for use as housing; we called them "cans." They were scarcely big enough for one person, so of course there were two of us in each one.

We were given two days to settle into our cans and get used to the base. I developed a hatred for TQ quicker than I thought I would. The computer and phone centers were always busy, everything was at least a ten-minute walk away, there were no trees, and the base was on a plateau so it was always windy.

Once I had sufficiently cemented my hatred for my new home, I was put to work. My first job was a daily eight-hour shift searching the contracted trucks running supplies from Kuwait. The job was hateful. My entire day consisted of a long nap that was constantly being interrupted. I'd wake up, put on sixty pounds of gear, and climb in and out of semi tractors. So began my extension.

CHAPTER 28:
Baghdad

A
BOUT TWO WEEKS AFTER WE GOT TO TQ, Horn and I were sent to Baghdad to testify against Fat Hassel. After a little more than ninety minutes on a CH-47 helicopter, we landed on the airstrip next to the American embassy in Baghdad. It was 0115. The cool night air blowing through the gunners hatch up front and out the open back ramp had kept everyone onboard just miserable enough to stay awake.

We collected our bags, left the landing zone in a single file line, and were turned loose in front of a small building without any instructions. This small morsel of freedom was not only unwelcome, but also more frustrating than when our own command treated us like toddlers. Being sent to a new place for an important assignment seemed like a good time to start holding our hands and making sure we knew what was going on. It is a perfect example of the kind of reasonable thinking that brings the military to a screeching halt.

So there we were, in Baghdad with no idea what to do. I followed Horn into a building to see if we could get a few answers. The soldiers working there had none, which met our expectations. Horn did remember that he had been given a phone number to call in the event that we needed help. I slumped into a chair and took a short nap while he roused an air force tech sergeant out of bed with his call.

Less than five minutes after I had sat down, Horn woke me from a dead sleep. I followed him out of the building and through a small maze of fifteen-foot-tall concrete barriers that led out onto a dimly lit sidewalk. Saddam's presidential palace, lit up like a Wal-Mart at Christmastime, stood on the other side of a concrete fence that ran parallel to us across the street. The gate in the wall was guarded by Peruvian contractors who were much more polite than the Ugandans we dealt with in Fallujah and TQ. We had to clear our weapons and show our ID cards before they would let us inside the palace compound.

We followed the sidewalk around to the back side of the palace, as Horn had been instructed, and waited outside the KBR (Kellogg, Brown, and Root, a subsidiary of Halliburton) housing office. The air force tech sergeant met us after a fifteen-minute wait, during which Horn had to empty his hyperactive bladder twice.

The airman led us inside the palace and up to the Judge Advocate General (JAG) office to do some paperwork. He told us what to expect while staying in Baghdad over the few days. The most notable thing he said was that it had been almost two months since the last incoming mortar or rocket, so it should be a pretty nice vacation for us in comparison to Anbar. We finished the paperwork in twenty minutes and the airman told us to go back to the KBR housing office to sign in, draw linen, and get a tent assignment.

The woman working in the housing office seemed entirely too jovial to be working in Iraq at 0230. She got us some pillows and sheets, asked us to sign a roster for tent number five, and handed us a crude color-coded map of the bus routes. She sent us out the door with incomplete directions to tent five and cheerfully retreated to her laptop to resume whatever it was that we had interrupted. I figured she was surfing some lesbian butt-fisting porn sites, since that would be about the only thing on the internet that could put me in such a jovial mood at 0230.

We went on our way with arms full of bedding, bags, and our weapons. It was 0300 before we found our temporary residence and claimed our beds. We slept until about 1200 the next day and ate at the chow hall right behind the palace, next to the pool. It was the best food I'd eaten in months. After lunch we walked around the area outside of the palace compound. There were a couple of Iraqi shops and a couple of American fast food joints. We stopped at our tent to drop off the shit we bought before going to our 1500 meeting with the JAG lawyer.

It was a short walk from our tent to the main entrance of the presidential palace. We walked across a small lawn into a parking lot filled with people going about their day. A few SUVs were parked along the front of the building to our left, and there were a couple of groups of birds eating in the lawn to our right. Altogether it presented a quiet and peaceful scene.

I was just starting to relax when a loud screaming sound, unlike anything I've ever heard, shredded the quiet in much the same way that a screaming toddler can ruin a Memorial Day service. The sound gave just enough warning for me to formulate the phrase "oh fuck," but not quite enough time to vocalize it. I got the "oh" out, but just as my lower lip hit my teeth to make the "f" sound, there was a loud explosion about twenty meters to our right, smack dab in the middle of the lawn where the birds had been grazing.

I hit the ground, then decided a better option would be to get out of the parking lot in a hurry, so Horn and I got up and ran behind a Toyota Land Cruiser. In hindsight I realize that the open parking lot would have been a better choice for the simple fact that for the next three days, I had to listen to Horn babble about how hiding behind a Toyota during a rocket attack would help him sell cars when we got home. He was a salesman at a Toyota dealership in his civilian life.

Once we were relatively safe behind the Land Cruiser we surveyed the situation, which could best be described as total chaos. Some people were on the ground, while others ran around with no apparent destination. Only a few people had the presence of mind to hide behind any type of cover. I looked over to the main door of the palace, now only about fifty meters away, and saw a woman standing in the open doorway, motioning us to make a run for it. Horn saw the same woman and led us into the safety of the palace.

Inside the palace, as my adrenaline began to fade, I realized that somehow my elbow had been hurt in the attack. A sharp pain burned up the back of my arm while my forearm felt cold and wet. I told Horn that I thought I was hit with shrapnel, though later I realized that the arm that hurt was not the one facing the explosion.

Horn held my rifle while I took off my blouse to examine my elbow. I looked at my arm for a bit, finding only a bruise on my elbow and a dent in my self-esteem. Horn hurled a tirade of insults at me when he saw that I was not really hit. I put my blouse back on and decided that I must have hit the butt stock on my rifle when I was getting on the ground.

When we regained our composure, we went up to the second floor of the palace to the JAG office for our meeting. The office was filled with a light haze and smelled of burnt gun powder. One of the lawyers started to tell us about what had happened and that the windows in the office had been open, so smoke had blown in. We explained to the lawyer that we were the closest people to the rocket when it landed.

The people working in the office took a strong interest in our close call, asking a bunch of questions and listening to our responses with fascination. I thought everyone around there was a little bit too excited because it was just a normal Saturday, after all.

When Horn met with the JAG, naval First Lieutenant Stern, I eavesdropped on their conversation from the other side of the room, where I was entertaining myself by looking at the pictures and maps hanging on the wall. Stern looked at Horn and asked, "What can I do for you, gentlemen?"

"We flew in last night and were told to come to this office and check in for a court case on the 26th for Haythem Kudar Muhammad," Horn replied.

The lieutenant turned to his desk and started digging through a pile of paperwork and folders, mumbling something we couldn't make out before giving up less than a minute later. "Are you sure you guys are here to see me? Where are you stationed?"

If Horn had just answered the question, "Where are you stationed," we would have saved a lot of time and bother. Instead, he explained to the lawyer, "An air force tech sergeant told us to come to this office at 1500 and find First Lieutenant Stern."

When Horn finally answered the man's question and told him we were stationed in Anbar Province, the navy officer figured out that we were indeed in the right place, but were talking to the wrong lawyer and would have to come back the next day to see Captain Hirsch. The confusion was due to uniform discrimination. Lieutenant Stern saw that we were army and assumed that our case belonged to him. Apparently the airman from the night before had made the same mistake. The case actually belonged to Captain Hirsch, who was the JAG for all of the cases coming out of Anbar Province, which was occupied almost entirely by marines.

With most of our day wasted thanks to uninformed assumptions, Horn and I left the palace to explore the rest of the misleadingly named "Green

Horn, a car salesman at a Toyota dealership in his civilian life, stands next to a shitty Toyota SUV in Iraq. Always looking on the bright side of things, after the rocket attack Horn said, "I could use this to sell cars!"

Zone." Green Zone sounds like a peaceful place filled with meadows and happy creatures; Baghdad's Green Zone was more like a living hell, as we would learn before we left. We found a bunch of shops about a ten-minute walk from the palace. I bought a camera, a pair of knock-off Nike shoes, and a bootleg DVD box set containing the entire *The Simpsons* series. We walked into a massage parlor, thinking a happy ending might be a pleasant diversion. We promptly left, though, when we saw the man who was giving the massages was a little too flamboyant for our tastes, even though we may well have gotten the happy endings we desired.

We kept exploring the area after we dropped our merchandise off at our tent. We took a walk in another direction and found a large recreation center.

There was a gym with treadmills and weights in one wing, and in the other there was an aerobics class with a lot of good looking women in the front and a bunch of creepy looking guys in the back. Outside there was a large pool that was too cold to swim in and a tent with a couple of foosball tables and some pool tables.

I let Horn win a couple of games of foosball before shifting gears and destroying his ego with a couple of severe ass-kickings. (Later I learned that spinning the players to launch the ball to supersonic speed is bad foosball etiquette, but since Horn didn't know this I was able to use the technique to good effect.)

People started to filter into the tent for a weekly salsa dance. Camp Fallujah had had a salsa night, but it was cancelled shortly after we got there. An officer realized that boys and girls were touching each other and had it done away with. We spent the night ogling the women on the dance floor and wishing that we knew how to salsa dance. We caught a bus that took us back to our tent shortly after the dance ended.

I was startled awake the next day by an explosion in the distance. It was a VBIED at one of the gates to the Green Zone. It was more than a mile away and still shook me out of my sleep. As I got up and prepared for my day, I heard another rocket land on the other side of the palace. It destroyed a living container similar to the one I lived in at TQ.

Horn and I went into the palace to look around after lunch. We took a few pictures around the building and were scolded by one of the Peruvian security guards for photographing a sensitive area.

Another rocket landed a few minutes before we were going to meet with the lawyer. Fifteen people eating lunch on the patio outside of the chow hall were injured.

Captain Hirsch met us in the coffee shop with May, the 'terp who would be working with us during the hearing. The idea was for us to be comfortable with each other so that everything would be smooth and professional in court.

We sat down at our table after being introduced to May and getting scolded by Captain Hirsch for calling her a 'terp. Apparently both "'terp" and "interpreter" are insulting to anyone who translates Arabic into English. We corrected ourselves by calling her by what we thought would be a more politically correct term—"translator"—but found this to be only slightly more acceptable than 'terp or interpreter. "Linguist" was the word we were apparently looking for to appease the POG lawyer and her 'terp.

Once everyone was satisfied with his or her title, we started to talk about the case. We went over the procedures for testifying in an Iraqi court, what to expect from the judge, and we got our story straight.

When Captain Hirsch finished, she told us that we could relax the next day and meet her the day after in her office at 0700. She thanked us and went to finish her work for the day. We took some time to check our email before chow.

We ate on the patio near the area where the rocket had hit earlier that day, figuring that lightning doesn't strike the same place twice. In the middle of our meal, a group of about twenty people gathered in an open tent on the other side of the courtyard behind the palace. They were employees of the State Department who were allowed to drink as long as they were not armed. I told Horn that it would be nice to see a rocket tear through their tent so we could run off with their booze.

We hung out near the pool most of the night waiting for just such a rocket but eventually I got bored, so I signed up for a ping-pong tournament. While I awaited my turn, I watched an air force girl play for an hour, paying very close attention to the way her chest jiggled every time she swung her paddle.

I was put into the second game against a very quiet Arab man. He won first serve and the game started. I felt confident in my ping-pong abilities because I grew up with a table in my basement. I didn't realize that I would be playing against an Arab Forrest Gump. He kept a calm and stern look on his face while he hit a perfect curve ball on every shot. In a best-of-three series, I lost the first two games, scoring a collective seven points spread total both games.

After being humiliated, I sat down next to Horn and prepared to be ridiculed, but he didn't get a chance to torment me about my embarrassing defeat because another rocket flew over our heads, making that same god-awful sound. It sounded like it landed close to us, but we couldn't figure out exactly where it landed because there was no detonation.

We sat in our chairs, chuckling at the people lying on the ground. Everyone there had assumed the classic duck-and-cover position that school children were taught would save them in the event of a nuclear attack during the Cold

War—everyone except two marines who sat at another table, casually smoking cigars. They reacted the same way we did to the rocket. We went over to find out why they didn't hit the ground like the rest of the people in the courtyard. They told us that they were stationed on Camp Habbaniyah and were used to dealing with incoming. We told them we were stationed in Camp TQ, just down the road from Camp Habbaniyah. We had a nice chat with the marines, talking about IEDs, mortar attacks, and other charming aspects of life in Anbar Province.

The next day, I again slept into the afternoon. Once again, I was awoken by explosions in the distance. Horn and I got on a bus and went sightseeing. We saw the famous Cross Sabers and the Tomb of the Unknown Soldier. Riding the bus was an uncomfortable experience. We felt naked without our body armor. We rode around the Green Zone among the general public, and no one thought it was strange except for us. We were told that everyone in the Green Zone is searched before they can get in.

After dinner we went to the movie theater and watched *Tango and Cash* before going to bed early. We wanted to be rested and ready for court in the morning.

The next morning we were both up before the alarm went off. Neither of us had slept well with the day in court hanging over our heads. We went into the palace to meet the lawyer and get our body armor.

About fifteen of us gathered behind the palace for a patrol brief. We stood in a circle while one of the lawyers showed us the route we would be taking to the courthouse. We also went over some drills for reacting to a sniper and evacuating a casualty from hostile fire.

One of the lawyers got a phone call near the end of the briefing. It was a wrong number dialed by an Iraqi. She told him in English that he had the wrong number and that she couldn't understand him, then hung up. It was apparent that he didn't understand when he called back, so the phone was given to one of the 'terps—or rather, linguists—to get rid of the caller.

We climbed into a group of armored Chevy Suburbans and drove to the other side of the Green Zone, where we were dropped off. Once out of the Suburban, we were told to load our rifles for the walk inside. The courthouse was about two hundred meters outside of the Green Zone and was known to be a magnet for sniper fire.

Inside the building, we took our body armor off and unloaded our rifles. All of our gear was locked in a room guarded by an MP. It was uncomfortable walking around unarmed, especially when we saw that the judges' Iraqi bodyguards had pistols slung under their arms.

We were given a tour of the building by an Iraqi tour guide named Mustaff. He told us that he was born and raised in Iraq but moved to San Diego about thirty years ago. He had come back after the Iraqi government was set up to help his country rebuild. Mustaff worked for the Iraqi court as a linguist, helping to prosecute insurgents.

The building that became the Iraqi courthouse was built by Saddam as a museum to house the gifts he received from other world leaders. It was explained to us that the Iraqi court worked almost identically to the American courts, except that the jury was replaced by four extra judges.

After the tour we were brought to the office where the pretrial hearing would take place. I was instructed to stay outside of the office while Horn gave his testimony, so that I wouldn't be able to hear what he said. I sat outside the door of the office trying to talk to the four bodyguards who worked for the judge inside. We couldn't communicate very well, but still managed to have a good time. I'd heard that people in Baghdad commonly believed that people from Fallujah were simple-minded, so I teased one guy that he was from Fallujah. He was offended, but his three friends laughed at him until I told one of them, using some intricate hand signals, that he was gay with the guy from Fallujah.

Now I just had two of them laughing. Things continued this way for almost thirty minutes. Horn was talking a lot, even though our lawyer had told him that Judge Ali got annoyed with people who didn't get to the point. I was called in by Captain Hirsch and I said goodbye to my new friends.

When I got into the office I was seated next to the defense lawyer. I was surprised that the defense lawyer was an Iraqi woman. I was even more surprised that she smelled nice. She'd covered her face with white powder and looked like some sort of ghost. I couldn't look at her too long because I was afraid that if I did, I wouldn't be able to stop gawking at her freakish clown makeup. Horn, Captain Hirsch, and the linguist/'terp sat across from me with the judge at a large desk immediately to my right.

I was sworn in and repeatedly asked by the judge not to lie. He asked me about everything that I had written in my report after we captured Fat Hassel.

I was asked to point out on a map which rooms we found weapons in and to describe what the weapons were. I started listing things and was told to slow down so that the transcriber could keep up. Judge Ali said that he wasn't used to getting a straight answer so quickly, after listening to Horn drone on endlessly about things he was not asked about.

I was asked to identify the defendant, who was sitting behind me next to an armed American MP on a couch. When I saw him, I again regretted not pulling the trigger on my shotgun the night of Operation Three Swords. I told the judge that he was the man that I had captured the night of the raid. He asked me to look again to make sure it was him. I looked and said that I was sure it was him, and was once again reminded not to lie.

Once I had satisfied the judge, Fat Hassel was taken out of the room and put back into the holding cell. Horn and I went to the room with our rifles and waited outside the door until everyone else was done with their cases.

We left the courthouse the same way we had entered it and unloaded our rifles before getting back into the Suburban. The ride back was made miserable by Captain Hirsch and another lawyer, Captain Armstrong, complaining about being extended. Both women were in the air force and had been extended for less than a month. They would serve a total of five months in Iraq before they went home. They quit bitching when we told them that we had just started our four-month extension and that we had already been in-country for a year.

We were done with everything we had to do in Baghdad when we got back to the palace. We caught the very end of lunch before going back to the tent to take a nap for the afternoon. Our scheduled flight back to TQ was still two days away, so we would be on vacation in Baghdad.

After a couple hours of light sleep I was again woken by explosions. They were not very distant this time. There were three or four explosions, so I figured that the insurgents were done for the day and I started reading a book. Less than ten minutes later, I heard the loudest, most horrible incoming rocket sound I had heard so far. It flew over our tent and slammed into the palace just outside the door of the tent.

Before I even heard the explosion, some shrapnel hit me in the head just in front of my right ear. Without thinking, I dropped to the floor and rolled under the bed. When my senses came back, I realized that I may as well get back up because a mattress wasn't going to help me if a lucky shot hit our tent. I might as well not die looking like a little girl hiding from the boogeyman under the bed.

When I sat up, I told Horn that I was hit while I held my head. It felt like I had been hit in the temple with a baseball bat. Horn called me a fag and told me to quit being a pussy. I showed him that I was serious and, when he saw the trickle of blood on my head, he apologized for not believing me.

After I concluded that my wound was nothing more than something I could inflict with my shaver, I went outside to see what was going on. There was a large chunk of one of the pillars missing, and smoke from the explosion was slowly floating away.

I gathered some shrapnel lying on the ground, along with a few small pieces of the palace. When I looked up there was a man in a suit pulling a small suitcase. He looked curious but seemed to be completely clueless about what had just happened.

"What's going on here?" he asked me.

"A rocket just blew a big-ass hole in that pillar," I explained pointing to the hole.

"Oh my god, that's my office!" he shrieked before running to the nearest door to the palace.

I laughed at him on my way back into the tent. Horn and I started talking about all of the close calls we were having in this shitty place and decided to try and get a flight out that night.

We started packing our shit when I noticed a small hole in the shoebox sitting on the bed between Horn and I. A piece of shrapnel had hit the box and sucked out all of the tissue paper on its way through before imbedding itself into the mattress underneath. We did our best to map its trajectory and found that if it had been roughly a foot higher it would have hit Horn in the head where he was sleeping.

We went to the helicopter pad as soon as we finished packing and got on a flight out later that night. It took us nearly two hours to fly back, but we were happy to be out of Baghdad.

CHAPTFR 29:

Operation Unnecessary Dangerous Stuff

I N Camp Fallujah we'd been terrified, we'd been exhilarated, and we'd been devastated. In Camp TQ we were just bored out of our fucking skulls. Our work consisted of sitting in towers staring at nothing for hours on end, or else searching trucks entering the gate. Other than that, all we had going for us was relentless masturbation and video games. I had an Xbox 360 and Yogi had a Nintendo Wii. I got extremely good at *Guitar Hero II*, *Need for Speed Underground*, *Call of Duty 3*, and spanking my monkey without making too much noise. The only thing that broke up the horrible monotony of our work at TQ was when we were occasionally sent back to Fallujah for another large operation. I went on two of these missions, one in early April and one in mid-May 2007.

On the first mission, we brought with us Specialist Brandon Foldoe and Private First Class Tyson Evans. They were both soldiers who joined my squad in March after we moved to TQ. They were replacements for Dunna and Corey.

It took four months for the replacements to get to us because, in his sublime incompetence, the Elicerio brought a barebones brigade to Iraq without any plan to deal with casualties. Finally, after four months, our squad was back to full strength.

When we returned to Camp Fallujah, we expected the mission to be this horrible dangerous expedition through the heart of the city of Fallujah and into the heaviest combat of the war. It turned out to be uneventful and boring.

We left TQ one morning after Spineless Six gave a short speech about how great we were, with a quick reminder at the end to stay safe. The drive was slow as usual.

I saw the bridge in Fallujah that the contractors were hung from a few years earlier. It appeared to be unused. The city itself was almost empty. The streets were lined with shelled-out buildings. The only thing I saw in the city that wasn't completely destroyed was the mosque. It was a beautiful building with only a few bullet holes in it.

The people looked at us with dead eyes as we drove through. They looked defeated and hopeless. There were no children playing in the streets like we had seen in the villages that we passed through before we got into the city. The whole scene was eerie and sad. Once we were out of the city, it took us only a few more minutes to get to Camp Fallujah. It was nice to be back at our old camp; I felt like I was home.

The next day we got our mission. We were there to patrol the desert to the east of camp. It was part of our old AO and was such an insignificant piece of real estate that we rarely patrolled it then. We sat out there and did nothing for hours on end. It was extremely pointless.

One day Horn ordered Foldoe, who was already beginning to annoy us with his constant complaining, to drive the humvee. He had never driven a humvee in Iraq and was so upset over having to drive us out to the desert so we could stare at nothing that he seemed close to tears.

"I won't drive," he whined. "I just can't do it. I don't want to get blown up."

"Don't worry about it, man," Horn assured him. "We are going into the desert. There aren't even roads out there. You could run around naked and nothing would happen to you."

"I just really don't want to. I can't."

"Well, you don't have a choice."

Foldoe drove the truck, but he was obviously not happy about it. He bitched almost nonstop for the rest of the day about how he sucked at driving and how he shouldn't have been forced to do it. When he wore that subject out, he started complaining about being in Iraq.

The mosque was one of the only things that still looked nice in the city of Fallujah.

"Oh, fuck you, man," I said. "You have been here for a fucking month. I am not bitching about it and I've been deployed since 2005. I don't want to hear any more of your whining."

The rebuke shut him up for the day, but the next day he started his mewling again and didn't stop for the rest of the deployment. He was by far the bitchiest person in our squad though he had no right to bitch. He was surrounded by people who had been dealing with the same shit for over a year and a half longer than him.

We kept patrolling the desert, searching for a group of people suspected of arms trafficking through there. We didn't see a soul the entire time. I flew

Joe Ness gets held down and pink bellied.

the Raven a couple of times while we were out there. I used it to help watch for the insurgent cell, but when I realized that we wouldn't find anything I started using it to buzz the other vehicles in the squad.

The one day when the platoon finally did something cool, I had the day off. A high value person was spotted at a gas station we were watching and the platoon raided it, catching the second most wanted person in Anbar Province. He had killed a few guys in an army unit stationed at Camp Fallujah.

A few days after the capture of the guy at the gas station, we were sent to Karmah, a small city northeast of Fallujah that had recently become a stronghold for insurgents. All in all, it was a pretty shitty place to be.

When we drove into the town we met two bongo trucks with DShK (Dishka) 12.7mm heavy machine guns mounted on them. The armed trucks

A bombed out building in Fallujah

belonged to the local militia, which took the heavy guns from insurgents who tried to attack the village. The insurgents mired the trucks in a muddy, swampy area and abandoned them. The villagers towed them out when the insurgents retreated.

The local militia formed in response to the recent surge in insurgent activity in the village. The locals got sick of al Qaeda trying to run the show, so they banded together and formed a militia to kick them out. We became the enemy of their enemy, so they began working with us. We were in the village to support them in case the guys who abandoned the trucks came back to get them.

We spent the day in the town providing security. The entire experience was strange, because there were Iraqis with guns walking around all over but they were not hostile. It was encouraging because the locals were finally taking matters into their own hands and taking care of themselves. The sight made me think that maybe there was hope for these people yet.

After the trip to Karmah we went back to TQ. It was again a very slow and uneventful drive through downtown Fallujah. The streets were just as creepy as they were before, but we made it through all right.

265

We spent most of the mission not wearing our gear and playing cards.

After a few more weeks of sitting in towers watching either the barren desert around TQ or Lake Habbaniyah, we went back to Fallujah for another mission. We again left with the impression that we would be doing some extremely dangerous, wild shit but once again we were wrong.

The trip through Fallujah was again creepy but uneventful, and when we got there it was again nice to be home. The mission this time was to go north of Fallujah to control a section of land near Lake Tharthar. The intent of the mission was to provide security for the marines as they raided the area because it was being used as an insurgent training ground.

Up to this point, the mission was unofficially named Operation Impending Doom Two, Operation Over-preparation, and Operation Unnecessary Dangerous Stuff. We weren't crazy about going on any of these missions to

266

Blomgren plays with an abandoned anti-aircraft gun.

Fallujah because, after surviving a year there already, we thought we were just asking for it by going back there every month.

When we got out there, the mission turned out to be mostly lame. We set up a roadblock to keep people from traveling north into the territory that the marines were working in, only to have the people go around us. Once we realized that our presence was negated by another road a few miles to our east and that no one was going to fuck with us, we came up with a few other names like Operation Butt-fuck, Operation Pointless Roadblock, and Operation Unnecessary Busywork.

Still, for a few days, Blomgren was all wound up, jacked and ready for combat. We liked Blomgren and respected the fact that he was a competent lieutenant, but because he had not calmed down as quickly as the rest of us, he began to get on our nerves. As a result we came up with two more names: Operation Repeat Everything Seven Times and Operation Lieutenant is a Fucking Retard.

After a couple days Blomgren finally calmed down and we just hung out in the middle of the desert. The area we were in had a couple of shitty houses and was otherwise wide open. We told the occupants of one of the houses to clear out for a few days and used that as our firm base. Taking over houses to use as firm bases was standard procedure. For the most part we took good care of the houses, except if there was any food left in the house we'd eat it. Also we'd use their blankets and leave them on the floor, and without fail Grub would climb out on the roof and take a shit, but we didn't trash the houses or anything like that. This particular house was a great firm base because we could see people coming for miles around. Since we didn't have to worry about our security, we sat outside in our t-shirts playing cards and relaxing.

The mission lasted a little more than a week and we went back to TQ, happy to have once again avoided any kind of danger. The trip back was again nothing but eerie. I saw Fallujah for the last time. It was the last time I saw the walking zombies that the inhabitants had become. I didn't know this would be my last trip to Fallujah at the time, but if I had, I'd have been happy about not seeing that city again. Camp Fallujah was a different story. It had become like home to me.

CHAPTER 30:
Operation Kyrgyzstani Punani

I SPENT MOST OF THE REST OF THE DEPLOYMENT trying to stick my dick in a Kyrgyzstani girl who worked in a coffee shop on base. She was a tiny Asian girl, short and cute, and her English wasn't great. Yogi and I had a double-date with her and her friend. Yogi acted as translator (Russian is the primary language in Kyrgyzstan just as it is in Uzbekistan), but he fucked it up. He made some raunchy remarks to me that were supposed to be in English so the girls wouldn't understand, but then he forgot and said them in Russian.

It wasn't a complete disaster. The date went all right and we went out with them again a couple of days later. On our date, Venera (the girl I was dating) asked me to teach her English. We went to her can and got her English books, while Yogi and Medina went somewhere else and started fooling around. It turned out that I'd got the prim and proper Kyrgyzstani, and Yogi got the slutty one. We had three or four more dates, or rather study sessions, because all we did was study English. Yogi and his Kyrgyzstani fucked like hamsters. No matter how hard I tried, I never even got to put my arm around her. Eventually I got tired of it and quit hanging around with her. Yogi kept fucking his Kyrgyzstani for the rest of the deployment.

When we did patrols out of TQ, we'd drive into Kabani, a small village between the airbase and Lake Habbaniyah that seemed completely untouched by the war. We'd sit there for six to eight hours at a stretch in an attempt to

269

Kids in Iraq beg for food, water, and anything else they can get their grubby little hands on. The one in the hat stole Grub's *Cat Fancy* magazine.

create the illusion that we had a reason to still be in Iraq. While we sat in the village, we were constantly harassed by children.

They were different from the children in Fallujah. The Kabani kids seemed to have a sense of entitlement. The kids in Fallujah were just empty souls beaten down from years of war. The kids around Fallujah begged for food and water the same as the kids in Kabani, but they did so out of necessity—they really needed the help and weren't just trying to scam candy from us like the kids in Kabani.

The kids in Fallujah didn't like us as much as the kids in Kabani did.

The little bastards in Kabani were spoiled by the soldiers and marines who constantly patrolled there. They'd run up to the humvees in mobs of twenty or thirty, yelling and fighting with each other, trying to get candy and food from us. A few of the older kids would send younger kids to us and have them bring back their spoils. Then the older kids would divide up the sweets, keeping the best things for themselves.

Begging seemed to be the only pastime the kids had, and after a while it really started to grate on us. At one point Nelly got so sick of the begging that he started chasing the kids around yelling, "Mistah! Mistah! Need food for baby." The kids were so confused by the role reversal that they just walked away.

Max stands with Ben Slater and John Ecker. He is probably plotting how to get them into the trunk of the humvee as well.

Being the benevolent philanthropists that we were, we tried to make the begging a learning experience by giving the kids lessons in capitalism—we made them fight for money and food. We'd get two kids to beat the piss out of each other until one either started crying or ran away. The winner usually got a dollar or some food.

When the foodstuffs ran out, the kids would develop sticky fingers. They'd try to steal everything, from magazines (both the paper kind we read and the metal kind we stuck in our M4s) to parts of our uniforms. Grub lost a copy of *Cat Fancy* to the little shits. It was his favorite periodical and he was so devastated by the loss that he didn't speak to anyone for nearly a week after it went missing.

The squad poses for a picture for the Patriot Guard to say thank you for the commemorative shirts they are wearing in front of their company mural, while Yogi makes a statement about life in Camp Taqaddum by putting the barrel of his rifle in his mouth.

When the kids couldn't steal from us, they'd try to barter. Thorn managed to trade some of his less important gear for a slingshot.

A series of practical jokes by our interpreters didn't help our relationships with the kids. Max orchestrated the most memorable of these pranks. He gathered a couple of kids around the back of a humvee one day and told them that they could take all of the MREs and water that they wanted if they dug it out of the trunk of the humvee themselves. With the children foraging in the trunk, he shut the lid and trapped them inside.

I made seven dollars wearing those panties.

"*Ak ak badurka durk Mohammad jihad*," Max yelled into the trunk. "*Allah sherpa Mohammad jihad bak Allah daka*." Whatever Arabic gibberish he was yammering at the kids must have been pretty bad, because they went completely ape shit in the back of the humvee. After he'd delivered his horrible message to the kids, Max walked away, leaving them screaming in the trunk. He came over to us and explained what he had just done.

"I fucking told them that I was kidnapping them and that they would never see their families again," Max laughed over the screams emanating from the trunk. "They're fucking scared shitless."

Eventually, Max set the children loose. He gave them each a bottle of water and an MRE, and they all ran home as fast as their little legs would carry them.

In June most of the company went to Fallujah for one last mission while I stayed back to take my vacation in Doha, Qatar. The mission they went on was to provide security in the same area in which we'd conducted Operation Unnecessary Dangerous Stuff. They were supposed to provide protection for some engineers who were building a FOB called COP Golden. The acronym "COP" is something that I had never heard before. I assumed that it meant something like "combat outpost" or "center of philanthropy," or maybe it stood for "caressing our penises." I don't know why the marines didn't just call it a FOB like everyone else.

The mission was long and boring. The guys stayed in a bombed-out chemical plant used to manufacture pesticides and watched the desert. Watching the desert is just like watching the grass grow, except there is no grass. The only excitement occurred when one of the engineers who was making a berm around the new base hit a buried drum of pesticides with the blade of his bulldozer. When he hit it, a yellow cloud of chemicals was released into the air. The engineer freaked out and tried to get away by jumping off of his dozer. He hit his face when he fucked up his jump. When everyone saw his bleeding nose, they thought that it was bleeding because of the chemicals and freaked out. Eventually, they figured out what was going on and returned to normal.

The only other event that I missed seeing on that operation was Myrold almost shooting his foot off due to incompetence. While he was walking around with Jones and Hatton, he bent over and his rifle discharged into the ground just inches from his foot. A piece of his gear had caught the trigger and fired the rifle. Had Myrold not been an incompetent fuck, his rifle would have been on safe. Hatton and Jones reportedly just laughed at him. I was a little bit more concerned because the incident proved just how dangerous he really was to all of the men he "led."

While all of that fun was happening, I was enjoying a much needed vacation in Qatar. I went with Staff Sergeant Chris Lemke. Lemke was the squad leader for 3rd Squad before injuring his knee in training at Camp Shelby. He was replaced by Hatton and became the company's intelligence analyst once he recovered from his injury.

I was the last guy in my squad to go to Qatar for the simple reason that I was one of the only guys who wouldn't bitch about not having been able to go if we had run out of time. Just about everyone else was a complete whore for going on pass to Qatar, but I really didn't care one way or another. By

I express my feelings over a beer after someone asked me what I thought about the extension.

that time in our deployment, I no longer cared about much of anything. Yogi was the only other guy who didn't give a shit about going to Qatar, but that was because he was busy fucking his Kyrgyzstani girlfriend up one wall of our can and down the other. Plus he had a stash of contraband Royal Horse whiskey, some rotgut booze that was so awful that its country of origin wasn't even listed on the label.

So, while everyone was out doing shitty work in the heat of the summer, I was drinking beer, eating at Chili's, and swimming in a military resort base.

Lemke and I went with a couple of guys from Alpha Company—Sergeant Billy Fisher and Sergeant Something or Other Wagner (I forgot his first

Lemke was asked the same question.

name). They were cool enough to almost make me feel bad about the mean shit the men in Bravo Company always said about Alpha Company, but not bad enough to make me ask the others to stop.

We went through a half-assed customs check on our way into the country and then boarded a bus to take us to the resort. When we got there, we sat through a long briefing explaining the rules. The consequence of breaking the rules was being sent out of Qatar into Iraq on the first available flight, regardless of the flight's destination. We would be responsible for getting ourselves back to our bases from wherever the flight dropped us off.

Once we heard all of the rules, which basically amounted to "Don't have any fun" (no drinking more than three beers per night, no hard alcohol, no sex, no drugs, no guns), we went to the pool and ate Chili's poolside. After a few hours of sitting in the pool, throwing a ball around, and ogling women, we went to the bar, which had just opened for the evening.

We sat down with a bunch of other Alpha Company soldiers at a table in the back of the bar and started drinking our allotted three beers. We drank a Danish beer called Tuborg because it had half a percentage point more alcohol in it.

I drank my first Tuborg and then switched to Fosters. I decided that if I wasn't going to get drunk, I might as well be drinking something decent. After a couple of beers, I loosened up enough to sing some karaoke. I dedicated *All Out of Love* by Air Supply to the Elicerio.

I sang the song as loud as I could and the entire place was repulsed by the squealing that I was passing off as singing. The table I was sitting at was the only exception. When I announced what song I was going to sing, someone went and found a half-dozen officers on the brigade staff. They stood in tears, laughing, while I sang a song professing my love for our knuckle-dragging Neanderthal commander.

After the song, I found two guys who were willing to sell me their beers at an inflated price. I paid the men and managed to get falling down drunk. I vaguely remember an episode that involved me running around in the bar wearing a pair of lacy pink panties over my shorts, but the details elude me.

That set the pattern for the next six days at Qatar. I would wake up at 1200, have lunch at Chili's, drink until 0400, go to sleep, get up, and start the whole process over again. All in all, it was a pretty unremarkable week.

I went back to TQ and spent the rest of the month sitting at the camp gate, looking at the gravel and sand. By that time we had watched every decent movie on base, so we resorted to watching mind-bogglingly stupid chick flicks like *The Holiday* and *Wimbledon* and *Failure to Launch*. We were so bored that we watched that last movie, which has to rank among the most insipid films ever created, five times. The fact that we watched this simpering idiot fest five times even though we didn't get to see Sarah Jessica Parkers' tits, much less her furry brown yodel patch, provides an accurate metric by which to measure our boredom.

They moved us into some poorly constructed wooden huts with malfunctioning air conditioners for about a week and a half while we waited for a plane home. We slept twelve to a room in a room that wasn't big enough to house six people. Or rather, we tried to sleep—without functioning air conditioners it was about 120 degrees in the rooms, which made it damn hard to sleep.

We didn't have any assignments for the entire week and a half, so we had nothing to do but beat off and play video games in the rec center. I played *Halo* at least eight or nine hours every day.

On July 16 we finally got a plane home. We loaded our gear on a big-ass C-17 that had airline-style seats in the cargo bay, so it was more comfortable than the plane that had brought us to Iraq.

The plane taxied out on the runway, the jets kicked in, and as soon as the wheels left the ground everyone started cheering. It felt great to be leaving that fucking country.

CHAPTER 31:
Sticking a Shiv in Hugo Chavez

"WE WILL BE LANDING IN BANGOR, MAINE, in just a few minutes to refuel," the captain of the plane said over the intercom. "We will be on the ground here for about an hour to refuel for the last leg of our flight to Volk Field in Wisconsin."

The mood in the plane was bordering on pee-pants giddy. We would finally all be back on American soil for the first time in almost a year and half.

When we landed, we walked through the airport and met the Bangor greeters, a large group of people who gathered at the end of the hallway every day to cheer and thank the soldiers coming from and going to Iraq and Afghanistan. It was a gauntlet of handshaking and hugs that was almost overwhelming.

At the end of the gauntlet was the airport terminal. I was pointed in the direction of a room where we could use cell phones that were donated by some local organizations.

"Mom, I'm home," I told my mother when I got on one of the phones.

"What?" my mom asked, already starting to choke up and cry.

"I'm in Maine. I'm back home in the States."

"Oh my god! I'm so happy, I can't even believe it."

"I'm going to get off of the phone so someone else can use it. I'm sure you'll be more than happy to call everyone and tell them that I'm back."

"Yeah, I can do that. I love you."

"I love you too, Mom." I hung up and handed the phone to the next guy in line.

After my phone call I went to the small convenience store to buy a magazine and some junk food to enjoy for the last leg of the flight. I left the shop with the latest copy of *The Economist* magazine, *A Man Without a Country* by Kurt Vonnegut, a bag of Peanut M&M's, and a pair of cigars for me and Grub. Well stocked up with provisions, I went to chat with some of the World War II vets who were there greeting us.

The guy I ended up talking to had some interesting war stories to tell, until I realized that he was somewhat senile. After he ran out of war stories he started over, talking to me like we had never met, and told me the same stories over again. I was trapped in a cycle that ran three times before I was saved by a photographer. She took a picture of me sitting next to the guy, breaking his endless loop of stories.

Winnie sat down next to me after the photographer left. Seeing my opportunity to escape from hearing the same stories for the fourth time, I excused myself to go to the bathroom and left Winnie to deal with the old vet. Once I was away from him I wandered around the terminal until it was time to get back on the plane.

On the flight, I read the entire Vonnegut book and took a short nap before waking up when the captain announced that we were about to land at Volk Field. Lieutenant Blomgren told me that Kriesel would probably be waiting for us when we got off of the plane.

As the plane dropped out of the sky, it bounced and shook, intensifying my nervous anticipation. I was so excited to be home that I was shaking by the time we touched down.

When we taxied to the stair car (the vehicle driven by the Bluth family from *Arrested Development*), I saw Kriesel standing on the edge of the tarmac waiting to see us. When we stopped they announced that we would be directed into the hangar to turn in our weapons. Then they asked the baggage detail (which included me) to stay and unload the luggage from the belly of the plane.

"Fuck! There is no fucking way that I am going to sit back here while everyone else gets to see Kriesel," I said, upset that I was being held back from seeing my friend for the first time since Dunna and Corey died. "They are fucking dreaming if they think that I will do that."

Miller drinks a couple of Heineken for the Marine Corps' birthday in November 2006. It was one of the few times we were allowed to have beer in Iraq.

"Hey Maurstad, I'll do your baggage detail for you," Evans offered. "Take my rifle for me."

"Thanks, man. This really means a lot to me," I said, taking his rifle.

When they opened the door I was one of the first people off of the plane, just behind some officers and Winnie. I hurried through the line of officers who hadn't been on the deployment but were eager to greet us anyway.

After I worked my way through the rash of insincere handshakes from the rear echelon motherfuckers, I hurried to be the first guy to see Kriesel, who waited for us a hundred yards away. I could see him standing on his two new prosthetic legs, leaning on two canes, with news cameras all around him.

"Pan! What's up, brother?" Kriesel greeted me with a huge grin.

"It is so good to see you, man," I said as I hugged my friend with tears in my eyes.

I let the hug go earlier than I wanted to because I was afraid of knocking him off of his fake legs. I didn't want to be the dick who knocked him down on TV.

After I finished hugging Kriesel, I walked into the hangar and turned in my rifle as well as Evans'. Not having my rifle made me feel vulnerable, almost naked. I found a seat on the other side of the big room and waited for my buddies to get in, so we could all hang out with Kriesel once he was done greeting everyone.

Soon Kriesel, his wife Katie, and his two kids Broden and Elijah were hanging out with our squad and a few other guys from 1st Platoon. We sat around joking and catching up on the eight months since we'd last seen Kriesel. The media circus following him everywhere he went was tough to get used to, but soon Kriesel's jokes had us all laughing hard enough to forget all about it.

Once the entire planeload of soldiers finished turning in their weapons, Major General Rick Erlandson, the commander of the 34th Infantry Division, gathered us all in front of his podium and gave a speech.

"You men have done a great job. . . . You were part of the longest deployed brigade in the history of the United States Army. . . . Readjustment is going to be difficult. You're coming home expecting to go back to normal, but you're going to find out that the normal you used to know doesn't exist anymore. You will have to find a new normal for yourselves. It will be a long, difficult process but I am confident that you can get it done. I'm going to ask you, as you go home, to go slow. Take it one step at a time. One hour at a time. A week at a time. A month at a time. But go slow. In closing, I want to thank you men for everything you have done and for your service. I wish you all a safe trip home and a successful transition back into your civilian lives."

After the speech, we were bused to Fort McCoy to spend the next week cooling off from Iraq and taking classes on how to deal with coming home and getting help if we needed it.

The next day we had nothing to do. The Fort McCoy reintegration bullshit didn't begin until the next day, so our commander got us a day at Noah's Ark water park in Wisconsin Dells.

While we were in the Dells, we were not allowed to leave the park, drink alcohol, or change out of our PT shorts. As anyone with a lick of common sense could have predicted, a large group of soldiers who had just returned home from the war in Iraq with an attitude of *fuck it, what are they going to do to me—send me back to Iraq?* should not be sent to a family water park the day after their return.

We rode to the Dells in three buses, one for each platoon. When we arrived, the other two platoons got off of the buses in their PT uniforms (which consisted of shorts, army t-shirts, and running shoes), but 1st Platoon all wore civilian clothes.

Myrold flipped. "What the fuck are you guys doing? Why aren't you in your fucking PTs?"

"We didn't know we were supposed to have them," a couple of guys mumbled.

"You mean none of you guys have any PTs?"

I've grown to believe that Homo sapiens can be categorized as either greater or lesser humans, depending on whether or not they have the capacity for abstract thought. Because we all knew that Myrold definitely fit into the "lesser human" category, we claimed to not have any PT uniforms, even though half of us did.

With no PTs, it was much more difficult to keep track of the platoon, since we were all wearing different things. This created the perfect conditions for us to leave the park and hit the town to get drunk and cause trouble. Within an hour we were in town drinking and raising hell, and it wasn't even noon yet.

Ecker, Thorn, Gallagher, Trontvet, and some other guys rented scooters and were tearing around town. The owner of the scooter company eventually saw them jumping curbs and doing burnouts with his scooters, so he took them away, ruining that fun. Grub was picked up by his fiancée and spent most of the day with her. Other guys in the platoon managed to find a bar that was open, so they started getting shitfaced almost immediately. Gallant, Hilligoss, and I had a more casual day, drinking a little at an Applebee's before seeing the live-action *Transformers* movie. I didn't much care for the movie, but in spite of his massive intellect, super-nerd Adam Gallant really seemed to enjoy the ridiculous premise that a car could morph into a giant battle robot.

After the movie, we went to the mini golf course next to the water park. I won the eighteen-hole round with a couple of lucky shots on two really big holes.

285

First Platoon Bravo Company as we left Iraq

It was almost time to leave by the time we got back to the water park.

When we walked back in, half of the company was hovering around the bar drinking. I had a couple of beers there before we had to start loading onto the buses to go back to McCoy.

I found Specialist Brock Havlicak passed out drunk on a beach chair near one of the pools. Brock—we called him "Spud" because he was from Idaho—was one of the replacements we got toward the end of the deployment. He replaced Jimmy in 1st Squad.

Moua, who was shit-faced drunk himself, helped me carry Spud to the bus. On the way to the bus, Moua told me that they had gone with some other guys to a Japanese restaurant and had drank sake until Spud lost consciousness. So Moua and the other guys carried Spud back to the park.

We eventually managed to round everyone up and get the bus moving back to Fort McCoy, but not before a few guys did some public urination on the side of the bus. We drove back to Fort McCoy in the highest spirits we'd been in since we were allowed to drink two beers back in November to celebrate the Marine Corps' birthday.

The next couple of days were slow, with a formation here and a class there. On our third or fourth day, Colonel Bristol and Sergeant Major O'Connell showed up. We had a formation to present the two men with some gifts from the company, including an engraved Ka-bar knife for each of them.

"This knife will have a proud place on the wall behind my desk," Sergeant Major O'Connell said of his knife. "Thank you, guys. I really appreciate this."

"As most of you know, I am going to South America tomorrow to do some work for a certain government agency," Bristol said after we gave him his knife. "I promise you that this knife will not be a virgin after this weekend. It will be strapped to my leg during this mission that I'm going on."

Bristol didn't give us any details, but we speculated that he was going to stick a shiv in Hugo Chavez's back, or something like that. The formation broke up and the entire company lined up to get a hug from Bristol and O'Connell. The two men had become father figures for the entire company. We weren't going to miss Iraq, but we were going to miss serving under Bristol and O'Connell.

CHAPTER 32:
Fatties Galore

WHILE SOME ASSHOLE LECTURED THE COMPANY about the consequences for breaking Fort McCoy's two major rules, most of us daydreamed about alcohol and leaving base to find some women. Unfortunately for us, the two major rules were no alcohol and no leaving base for any reason.

Once we realized what we were being lectured about, we began scheming as if the rules being presented were more of a dare than actual rules with any kind of attached consequences.

Yogi and I decided that the best time to get off base was during the company drinking night. Most of the company would be at McCoy's, the friendly on-base drinking establishment. While at McCoy's everyone would be required to remain in uniform and stop drinking at midnight. The army's fraternization policy would also still be in effect, which boiled down to: don't fuck army women (or army men, for that matter). Not that it would be difficult to avoid fucking army women; given a five-to-one male-to-female ratio, there just weren't that many army women to fuck.

Feeling that our chances would be better in La Crosse, Wisconsin, a college town just a sixty-dollar cab ride away, Yogi and I put on civilian clothes and got in a cab shortly after everyone had left the barracks for McCoy's.

After finding an ATM, we went to Hooters to start drinking. Our waitress was a short blonde named Beatta. She was a Polish exchange student going to college in La Crosse. Despite Yogi's Uzbek charm, she spent most of the night ignoring our empty pitcher of beer and talking to her boyfriend working in the kitchen.

Frustrated with the first waitress, Yogi bought dinner for two other waitresses in exchange for their company. The girls improved the aesthetics of the table, but stupefied me with their lack of intelligence. I feigned mild interest and let Yogi run most of the conversation.

Our third pitcher of beer ran out at the same time the girls decided they should stop sitting around talking to us. Yogi sensed my boredom and decided to call Token, who had skipped base and came to town earlier in the evening, and find some better entertainment. Token had given Yogi his cell phone and the phone number of a girl he had met a day or two earlier, saying that he would hang out with her until we were ready to hit the bars. We couldn't get Token on the phone, so after leaving four messages we gave up and went to find a better bar.

We went to an Irish pub about a block away. The jukebox was playing Flogging Molly at high volume and everyone seemed to be in good spirits. We took a table near the back after getting a couple drinks from the bar. There were no chairs, so the rest of the night looked like it would be a standing affair. After standing around a bit, two young women whom I thought looked very nice joined us. The conversation was much more interesting this time, but when the girls wanted to go to a different bar, Yogi bailed. He walked off on his own while I followed the girls to the next bar.

When we arrived I was given a green drink. I was skeptical at first and asked the name. It was called "swamp water" and I was told that the ingredients were secret. Somehow that explanation put my mind at ease and I downed the drink.

Not long after drinking the swamp water, I started to time travel. The next thing I remembered, I was dancing like an idiot at some other bar, and then getting thrown out of another bar for being drunk and belligerent. After I was thrown out of the bar, the girls told me that they were going to take me to their apartment to sleep for a little while and take me back to Fort McCoy in the morning.

The last thing I remembered before waking up in my bed the next morning was Yogi finding me. I was being dragged down the sidewalk with an arm around each girl. He set me down by a wall and told me not to move until he found us a cab.

The next morning while we were getting dressed, I asked Yogi about what had happened. He told me that I had taken off with a couple of fat chicks after he tried to get me to leave the Irish pub with him. He went bar hopping by himself while I was being dragged around by a couple of slam pigs.

Once dressed, we walked to the bus that was waiting outside of the barracks. The brain trust in charge of scheduling had not seen the obvious problems with holding our company's party on the eve of our first day of briefings. Like the rest of the company, I was still drunk when we were awakened the next morning at 0530. The briefings started with a small blood draw at 0600.

I sat in the chair next to the nurse when it was my turn. My head wobbled for a moment until I could focus my eyes. "I am going to be perfectly honest with you," I told the person tying a large rubber band on my arm, "there may be more alcohol than blood in that vial when you're finished." He chuckled as he prepared the needle. A combination of fear and queasiness forced me to look away when the needle drew close to my bulging vein. I gave a small jerk when I felt the needle touch my arm.

"Pussy," someone uttered under his breath when he saw my face tighten. I didn't recognize the voice and was too disgusted by the knowledge of a small piece of metal in my arm to look up and respond.

It all came to an end and I was dismissed into the auditorium. An usher of some kind caught me shuffling aimlessly near the back of the room and directed me to my alphabetical seat, which was between two people in my battalion whom I had never met before. Myrold was right behind me, with Nelson sitting next to him.

"What kind of sick fuck would let us drink the night before we have to start our briefings to get out of here?" I joked to Myrold and Nelson. The joke was not well received on the grounds that I had not shaven that morning and had still not cut my hair.

Myrold cut straight through the bullshit: "I didn't see you at McCoy's last night, Maurstad. Were you drinking with us?"

"I was in the back . . ." I said, turning around so my face didn't give away the lie. To avoid further questioning I let out a painful moan, put my head on the table, and tried to nap in the noisy room.

A few minutes later, the death-by-PowerPoint style seminar began, telling us it was okay to seek help, showing us where to go for said help, and telling us how to recognize that our buddies needed help.

We sat through PowerPoint presentations about shit no one cared about all day. That night almost everyone was hung over and most people stayed around the base, so Yogi suggested that we have the taxi cab pick us up away from the barracks to avoid raising suspicion. I found a suitable pick-up site two blocks away on the steps of a rundown, seldom-used building. We put all of our civilian clothes into my backpack and I told Yogi and Moua to follow me. A few other guys left base, too. Goldstein rented a pickup, so he left base pretty much every night, and Nelly rented a cabin in Jellystone Park, a tourist-trap family resort about ten miles from the base, and stayed there with Kriesel the entire time we were at Fort McCoy.

The taxi picked us up and we made it off post without incident. We drove the fifty-some miles into La Crosse and got dropped off at a mall.

We changed into our civilian clothes in a men's room at Sears. I wasn't happy with my apparel and decided to buy something better to wear at Pac Sun while Yogi and Moua went off on their own for a bit. I bought a new pair of plaid shorts, which Yogi immediately classified as "gay" when he saw them.

I waited for the others in the food court, our predetermined rally point. I was already hungry, so when an Asian man with a scraggly beard approached me peddling samples, I ate one. It contained mysterious meat with a strange texture. I thought it might be dog, but regardless, it beat the shit out of MREs. Soon I was holding a plate of the dog meat I had just sampled and was handing the cashier six bucks.

Moua showed up, saw that I was eating, and got his own plate of food. When Yogi came, we decided that once we finished off the food we should go to the Applebee's across from the mall and get a drink while waiting for a cab downtown.

When the cab arrived we left a small tip for the Applebee's bartender and took off for downtown. The cabbie was an older man with a long beard and long hair to mach. He looked like a lost member of Lynyrd Skynyrd who had just crawled out from under a bridge, and he creeped us out. He ignored us for most of the trip and didn't answer any questions, regardless of the volume in which they were asked. When he did speak, he talked about random buildings we drove by, explaining what they were and why they were significant. The three of us silently adopted a no-conversation policy and the cab driver was paid quickly when we stopped.

He dropped us off in downtown La Crosse and we went into the Helm Bar. Moua and I hung out and bullshitted with the bartender, while Yogi started hitting on some girl who was so depressed that listening to her tell her story to Yogi made me want to kill myself. We were relieved when Yogi disappeared with her, presumably to take advantage of her tragic state of mind.

We were still bullshitting with the bartender when Moua's phone rang. "Hey, where are you guys at?" Token asked from inside Moua's cell phone.

"We're at the Helm Bar in downtown La Crosse," Moua responded. "What do you need?"

"Who's with you?"

"Just Maurstad. Yogi left with some girl about thirty minutes ago."

"All right, I am in an apartment full of girls and they need some guys over here pretty bad. You guys in?"

Moua dropped the phone from his ear and repeated everything Token had said.

"Fuck yeah!" I shouted. "Let's go! Tell him to come pick us up."

After Moua finished talking with Token, we ordered one more drink and speculated about the women in the apartment with Token. The notion that there might be a very good reason these ladies needed help attracting guys didn't cross our minds.

Token rode up in a silver SUV just as we walked out of the bar. We got into the vehicle, encouraged by the sight of a very nice looking Korean girl in the driver's seat. We made a quick stop at a liquor store to pick up a couple of cases of beer.

Moua and I were left in the truck alone. We spent the short time discussing how hot the driver was and agreed that it would be really awesome if the rest of the girls looked like her.

I gave Token a thumbs up and mouthed the word "nice" when he got back in the truck. He looked away, trying not to let me see his shit-eating grin. Something was amiss.

We arrived at the apartment and I carried in a case of beer. Token was uncharacteristically quiet and I was getting worried. Moua still seemed clueless and excited.

When I entered the apartment I thought, *I'm going to need a lot more alcohol if this is going to happen.* Three women, each weighing in at a beefy 220 pounds or more, were sprawled out on the floor like beached manatees.

I sat down in the middle of the group and started drinking as much booze as I could get my hands on, hoping to black out before things progressed too far. I didn't know what was going to happen, but I knew it was going to get ugly and I didn't want to remember any of it.

Forty-five minutes later, I was lying on my back watching the ceiling spin. I'd almost achieved the correct frame of mind to harpoon one of these whales when one of them entered the merry-go-round of my field of vision. It was the medium-ugly one. "Get up and come to my room. We're going to fuck."

"I am not getting up, going anywhere, or doing anything with you," I slurred back. "If you want something, you are just going to have to figure it out for yourself."

She grabbed my arm and dragged me to her bedroom. "You're fucking strong!" I said, surprised to be on her bed.

"I don't fuck around. I see something I want and go for it," she said, trying to be sexy. She crawled into the bed next to me and started to touch me in ways that I had completely forgotten about.

I decided that it was time to swallow my pride and honor the long-standing national guard tradition of "porking a fatty." I started to work her clothes off while we made out. Things were starting to get going when she hit the brakes. "I feel bad," she said pushing me away.

"What's wrong?" I was annoyed that she was talking.

"Well, my friend really wanted to fuck you too, so I just feel really bad about doing this to her."

"Fuck it. Go get your friend."

"Really . . . "

"Yeah, hurry up," I said, urging her out the door.

Soon she returned with her friend at her side and I began to worry about the structural integrity of the bed we were occupying. I looked things over and discovered that there was no frame; it was just two mattresses on the floor.

With my safety concerns appeased, I coaxed the two of them into the bed and got things going again. The 220 pounds to my right started to dig around in my pants, while I tried to find the pussy on the 220 pounds to my left.

We were off to a running start again when the door opened. Moua walked in and stood in the corner quietly. Not having any issue with Moua being in the room, I decided to keep this information to myself.

"I think your friend's in the room," the sea cow on my right said.

"No, he just opened the door and left. Everything's fine, keep going," I encouraged.

"No," the dugong on my left added, "he's in the corner. I can see him and he's creeping me out."

"Moua!" I yelled. "What the fuck are you doing?"

"You know, man," Moua said in his heavy Asian accent, "just hanging out."

"You got to get the fuck out of here, man. You're fucking up my shit."

"No problem, bro," Moua said. He opened the door, stomped five times without moving, pretending to leave the room, and then stood quietly in the corner.

"All right, he's gone," I lied and went back to working the pants off the sea cow on my left, trying to find her pussy, which I never did find beneath the rolls of her belly.

"He's still in here," the one on my right said.

"No," I said, "he left."

"No, I can see him in the moonlight."

"Moua!" I yelled. "Get the fuck out of here!" This time he left for real.

So did the dugong on my left. "Fuck this," she said, "I'm done. I can't deal with this anymore." This left me alone with the manatee who had originally dragged me into the room, so I fucked her.

When we finished, she asked me to hand over her panties. When I saw the size of the massive garment in the moonlight, I realized I had to leave immediately. I threw on my clothes, grabbed Moua and Token, and got the hell out of there.

CHAPTER 33:
The Way Home

A T 0600 OF JULY 27, 2007, a fleet of charter buses pulled up outside our barracks to take us home. Everyone who was leaving on those buses had been waiting outside in the cool morning fog for nearly thirty minutes in a calm anticipation.

When the buses pulled up, we grabbed our bags and loaded them in the belly compartments. Once aboard our bus, we fought and pushed for seats like a bunch of piglets fighting for teats to suckle.

Once the bus was filled up, Staff Sergeant Howard went over some simple rules and our planned route. He said that we would stop at a couple of rest stops, but would not be stopping for food. When he finished he asked if we had any questions.

"Are we going to . . . ," Specialist Ness started a dumb question that was immediately met with a roar of insults from the group of sarcastic assholes who had gathered in the back of the bus, a group that included me. The answer to whatever question Ness had asked was met with a dumbfounded "no" from Howard.

After Howard answered Ness' question, all of us in the back of the bus did our best to mimic Ness' voice and mock him, asking the most ridiculous questions we could think of. Ness, always easily upset, stood up and yelled at all of us, "Fuck you guys! I can't wait to get off of this bus and away from you assholes." We laughed at him a little bit and told him that we knew he loved us as the bus started to move.

We left Fort McCoy and got onto the interstate. I fell asleep and woke up when we were leaving Wisconsin. The bus pulled into the first rest stop across the Minnesota border, where we took a break and met up with our patriot guard motorcycle escort. About fifty people were there waiting to be the first to welcome us back to our home state. When we got back on the bus I fell asleep again, waking up from time to time to join in on a joke.

The bus erupted in a roar when we spotted a Muslim woman walking into a bank in Pelican Rapids. Someone urged Specialist Corey Voecks, to open his emergency exit window and tackle her but it was a charter bus and the windows didn't open. Voecks, a communications guy, earned a Navy and Marine Commendation Medal for fixing a radio under fire when second platoon was out of ammo and just about to get its ass kicked at Pump House Flanders, allowing his squad to call in mortars and end the attack. I don't remember if he tried to open the window, or if he even paid much attention to the other guys, who were yelling obscenities at the Muslim woman and shouting ambush commands. I didn't get involved; my mind was elsewhere.

We continued on our way home, bickering with each other and trying to get in the last few insults of the deployment. People started to show up on the side of the road to welcome us home in Erskine, thirty miles south of Thief River Falls, our final destination. There were just a few cars on the side of the road in the small town. They honked, waved, and flew small flags to welcome us back.

The closer we got to Thief River Falls, the more people we saw cheering along the road. In Brooks, a helicopter joined the caravan, flying alongside the bus. Driving through the tiny town, I saw a sign marking the turn for Red Lake Falls, the home of Corey Rystad.

I started thinking about Corey, Dunna, and Jimmy. I thought about what happened and how they wouldn't be home like the rest of us. Most of all I thought about their families. I thought about them standing in a sea of people, surrounded by everyone else's happiness, mourning the absence of their own sons.

I put my head down on my knees and cried until we got to Plumber. I wiped my eyes the best I could in an attempt to keep everyone around me from realizing that I'd been crying.

Driving through Plumber, Gallant's hometown, we saw a lot of people out to support him beneath signs that read: "Welcome home, Sergeant Gallant!" This caused him to receive a barrage of ridicule. He told us to fuck ourselves while he looked out the window for his family, pointing them out as we drove past.

Once we were through Plumber, it was a quick cruise the rest of the way to Thief River Falls. We drove into town and were met by two school buses driving parallel with us on a frontage road. All of the people on the buses were hanging out the window waving at us.

The closer we got to the armory, the thicker the crowd on the streets became. We saw more signs and ridiculed each corresponding person. (Thankfully my sign was not spotted.) Everyone on our bus pressed against the window with a grin searching for family and friends in the crowd, pointing them out when we found them.

I spotted my evil ex-stepmother and pointed her out to the group in the back of the bus. The horrible woman was jumping up and down waving. When the bus was almost past her she pointed to me, said "There's Nick!" and started waving frantically.

How she spotted me through the tinted window was a mystery to me. I sat down to hold down my vomit and regain my composure. Once I was over the shock, the best thing I could figure was that she used her satanic powers to open an invisible demon portal to the bus, so she could look inside with her fiery-red Satan eyes.

I returned to the window, thankful that she did not manage to collapse my chest cavity in her attempts to steal my soul. I kept my eyes on the crowd, spotting a couple of friends along the way.

The bus pulled into the armory parking lot and drove through the narrow passage that was left by the exuberant crowd. We drove into the fenced-in area behind the building so we could get off of the bus without being crushed by the mob. We left our bags in the bus to be unloaded by a few members of the civil air patrol while we got into formation to march into the building.

The crowd let out a roar when we marched through the overhead door. The gymnasium-sized drill floor was packed wall to wall with yelling, crying, clapping, and smiling family members. A small area in the middle was left for

My mother, sister, and father greet me inside the armory in Thief River Falls, Minnesota.

us to march in and stand. Staff Sergeant Howard brought the group to a halt and called the thirty-nine soldiers to attention.

"Present arms!" Howard yelled, ordering us to salute, as a two-man detail lowered the flag signifying the end of our deployment. "Order arms!" He hollered after the flag was down. Then Howard shouted his last order: "Dismissed!"

I didn't think that one simple word could create so much chaos. The crowd cheered louder than they had before and swarmed our little group like we were Custer at Little Big Horn. Soldiers were attacked and nearly brought to the ground as their wives, girlfriends, and other family members located them. One by one, we each found our little family group hidden in the mob.

We were ripped away from each other to be carried off with our families to start our lives again. Suddenly the people I relied on and spent every waking minute with for the last twenty-two months were scattered, and I felt alone in a crowd of friends and family members.

My sister Katie was the first to muscle her way through the crowd and hug me. After her, I found my mother, followed by the rest of my family. I worked my way down the line hugging each of them and taking Katie along for the ride while she cried on my shoulder.

We moved toward the door to get outside and away from the mob, and then saw my grandparents and some other family members standing in the corner of the drill floor. I hugged them and talked to them for a minute.

I turned around to walk outside and spotted Brian Rystad in the crowd. I had been talking to him over the internet since Corey had died and had seen a couple of pictures of him.

I excused myself from my family, walked over to him, and gave him a hug. I asked him to bring me to his family, so we worked our way through the crowd to find the Rystad family standing quietly in a crowd of smiling people, just as I had pictured it on the bus.

I approached Jim and shook his hand, being a little too intimidated to hug him. I moved on to Corey's sister Sarah and started to choke back some tears while I hugged her.

"Thank you for being his friend," Corey's mother Donna said through her sobs. I hugged her, letting her cry on my shoulder for a minute or two. I was finally unable to hold back my tears and, by the time I told Donna that I had to go, I was crying very hard.

I turned away to find my family again and found my dad. He gave me a hug and tried to console me a little bit while I walked under his arm to the door. When we walked outside, there was another crowd cheering on each soldier as he walked out of the door. I walked down the lane they created, hearing a dozen "Welcome homes," "Good jobs," and "We're proud of yous." It seemed like a dream, walking through that group, still crying about my close friend who did not make it back.

We made it away from the crowd and met some more of my family and friends who were waiting for me outside. I gave more hugs and talked for a while, answering the same question over and over: "Yes, it does feel good to be home." In reality, I felt like shit because I missed my friends Dunna and Corey.

When I calmed down and was feeling happy again, my mom asked me if I would go say "hi" to a group of people who had come from the nursing home

Cousins Hunter, Hallie, and Ashley Skadsem are happy to have their favorite jungle gym back.

across the street. They were lined up in chairs and wheelchairs on the sidewalk holding a banner that said, "Welcome home B Co. 2-136!" I shook hands with the man at the tail end of the banner. He was wearing a World War II veteran cap, so I thanked him for coming to welcome us home and for his service to our country. I made my way down the line, thanking each one for being there before going back to my family.

Gary Barret walked out of the mob with tears in his eyes. Gary was a pastor at one of the churches in my hometown and had given me a lot of support through the deployment. I shook his hand and gave him a quick hug. We talked for a little bit before he wished me well and went to find another soldier with whom he had been in contact.

After Gary left I found my bags and packed them into my grandparents' van. We drove to my hometown of Newfolden, Minnesota. We went to the only bar in the town of 384, where more family and friends waited to see me. My brother Jay greeted me with a big hug and apologized for not making it to the armory to see me.

All of my family and friends gathered in the back room of the bar, ordered dinner, and talked. I had two whiskey and cokes before I started to spill everything all over the place. My family teased me a bit for being drunk and I protested, saying that I couldn't be drunk after only two drinks. I got another whiskey-Coke and immediately spilled it, ruining my argument.

The next couple of hours were spent telling stories and joking with my family before Jay and Nate Muzzy, who had been my roommate before I was deployed to Iraq, took me to Grand Forks to go drinking and celebrate my safe return home. It was July 27, 2007, and I wanted it to be October 1, 2005.

Epilogue

FOR THREE DAYS I HAVE SAT IN MY APARTMENT in downtown Minneapolis, Minnesota, with a completed manuscript for this book, and for three days I have been avoiding sending it to the publisher. My cousin and coauthor Darwin has been calling and emailing me—not only worried about what is happening with the book, but also for my well being.

To be perfectly honest, I am terrified to see this book published. I am worried that I didn't tell the story in such a way that will honor my friends. What I have written in this book is the story of me and my friends and it will be our legacy. The rest of us will be able to go on and make our own mark on the world while three of the finest men I have ever known—Bryan, Corey, and Jimmy—will live on only in the hearts of their loved ones and in this text. My biggest fear is that I did not do them justice in this book and will not have conveyed what they really were (and are): my heroes.

The completion of this story also means that I will be expected to be done with the war. I should be able to just move on with my life and forget about it. It means that readers will know our story. It also means that there will be veterans reading this. I know that I haven't been through much in comparison to most. I feel silly writing a war memoir having never killed a man or having never actually watched one of my friends die. I never even fired a single shot from my rifle in anger. I do not wish I had done any of those things, nor do I wish any other human being will have to do so, for that matter. I have watched those close to me deal with having killed and having fought to save their friends' lives, but having not experienced that myself it seems selfish for me to write about it.

My VA-appointed shrink tells me that I shouldn't marginalize what I went through just because others have had it worse. He tells me that I have just as much reason to need help as anyone else. I suppose I get to write the story of Bravo Company based solely upon natural writing talent alone, yet I still do not feel worthy of the task.

I suppose at this point it is just plain easier to publish the book despite my concerns. I just hope I have done our story justice. I hope that I have written something that Bryan, Corey, and Jimmy would have enjoyed and been proud of, and that their families will forgive me for the often graphic and horrifying nature of our story. I wouldn't have felt right doing this without including every ounce of pain. I hope that all of my brothers who came home with me will be proud of the way in which I told the story and forgive the jokes made at their expense. We were a bunch of kids thrown into a horrific situation and our humor, sophomoric as it may have been, was an important tool in helping us cope.

Speaking of my buddies, most have gone back to school since we returned. I was the best man in Grub's wedding just a few short months after we got home. He married a lovely woman named Jo, to whom I vaguely remember promising to bring her boyfriend home one night in Shelby when I was drunk off my ass.

Kriesel recovered from his injuries and can now get around quite well on his prosthesis. He was fortunate enough to have the support of many businesses and citizens in the Minneapolis-St. Paul metro area; they built him a brand new handicapped-accessible home in Cottage Grove.

Nelson is going to college part-time to finish up a degree while he works for Wells Fargo Financial. As I write this, he is also planning his wedding to Bryan's older sister Shannon McDonough in August 2008.

Horn is back at Walser Toyota in Bloomington, Minnesota, though he is no longer selling cars. He was promoted and is now doing financing and has his very own office. His wife is pregnant with their fourth child.

Kowalenko was sentenced to fifty months in prison, but the details surrounding the issue remain hazy. "Man, I just got drunk with the wrong people and made some bad decisions," he told me in a phone conversation from the Ramsey County Correctional Facility.

Neumiller was jailed shortly after returning home for allegedly stealing a safe containing twenty thousand dollars.

Ecker, Thorn, Micheletti, Pratt, and Moua are in college in Minnesota, while Yogi is in college in Phoenix, Arizona. Gallant is attending the University of North Dakota Law School in Grand Forks, North Dakota. Slater is working for Capital Computer Group, his father's company.

Joe Ness and Adam Seed went back to northwest Minnesota and both have babies on the way. Ness is starting his trucking business while Seed is finishing school to work for the Minnesota Department of Natural Resources.

Winnie went back to his old job at Digi-Key, an electronic component distributor in Thief River Falls, Minnesota, and is going to school part-time.

Jones continued his full-time job with the National Guard working as the company training coordinator in East St. Paul.

The last time I saw Myrold, he gave me a drunken speech about what a piece of shit I was and that I should just transfer out of the unit so he didn't have to deal with me fucking it up. Because of how the National Guard is structured, douchebags like Myrold get promoted in order to move them out of a unit. Myrold was promoted shortly after I left the company and is now a first sergeant with the battalion headquarters company.

Chris Ness is back in the Middle East, this time on a ship sitting in the Persian Gulf. Miller is back in his marine unit at Camp Pendleton, California.

Bristol and O'Connell are back in Fallujah doing the same thing they did last time, though I think O'Connell has moved out of Colonel Bristol's unit.

Max got a green card and is now a permanent resident of the United States. After a couple months living with a guy in third platoon he stayed on my couch in Minneapolis, Minnesota, for a month before deciding that it was too cold and moved in with a marine he knew in California. He begins college this fall with hopes of becoming a doctor.

I just finished a semester in college, and for the first time in my life I got decent grades. Compared to Iraq, school is easy. Working on this book has been hard; I've locked myself in my room for days at a time with nothing but a bottle of whiskey for company, but for the most part things are going all right. Since I've moved from northwest Minnesota to Minneapolis, I've transferred to Bravo Company 1-194, a company made partly from the remnants of the old Alpha Company that was lost to restructuring of the national guard, for the remainder of my enlistment. That should prove interesting once this book is published and they read all the horrible things I wrote about them.

Fortunately, most of the guys in Alpha Company are good soldiers and aren't any happier with the actions of some of their brethren than were those of us in Bravo Company.